GHOSTS AND LEGENDS
OF THE
PEAK DISTRICT

Kinder Reservoir from Kinder Scout

GHOSTS AND LEGENDS OF THE PEAK DISTRICT

DAVID CLARKE

JARROLD

About the author

David Clarke was born in Sheffield, and has been investigating and researching strange phenomena, folklore and tradition in the Peak District and Yorkshire since 1980. In 1990 he received an honours degree in Archaeology and Medieval History at Sheffield University, and is now reading for a higher degree in Folklore at the Centre for English Cultural Tradition and Language (CECTAL) at Sheffield University. His previous works include *Strange Sheffield: Folklore, Legends and Mysteries of Hallamshire* (with Rob Wilson, 1987) and *Phantoms of the Sky, UFOs: A modern myth?* (with Andy Roberts, 1990).

Acknowledgements

The author thanks the following for assistance in the research and writing of this book: the staff of the Local Studies Libraries at Sheffield, Manchester, Chesterfield, Buxton and Derby. Thanks for help and advice to Andy Roberts, Peter Naylor, Phil Shaw, John Davies, Martin Petch, Simon Crowe and Margaret Bellhouse; and to Claire for being there.

Readers wishing to report experiences of strange phenomena may contact the author at 6 Old Retford Road, Handsworth, Sheffield S13 9QZ.

Picture credits
Ashbourne News Telegraph: p.9; Chesterfield Library: p.26 (top), p.34, p.80 (top), p.93; Derby Central Library: p.7, p.49, p.51, p.54, p.58, p.105; Manchester Public Libraries: p.113; Sheffield City Libraries: p.46, p.59, p.80 (bottom), p.83, p.87, p.88, p.91, p.101

Front cover photograph of Chesterfield church by Charles Nicholas

ISBN: 0-7117-0555-0
© Jarrold Publishing 1991
Jarrold Publishing, Norwich
Printed in Great Britain. 3/96

Contents

Introduction . . . . *page* 6

Central Peakland

Ghosts and legends of central Peakland 15

Bakewell and district 20

Ghosts and spectres of the 'Plague Village' 24

Tideswell and district 32

Hob Hurst and Demon's Dale 34

The White Peak

Ghosts and legends of the White Peak 39

Stanton Moor – 'a lost world' 46

Headless phantoms of Peakland 53

Buxton and the South-western Moors

Buxton, Chapel-en-le-Frith and the western moorlands 57

Will o'the Wisp, UFOs and the Phantom Helicopter 65

The Curse of Dickey's Skull 69

The Phantom Dog of the Peak 75

Hope Valley and District

Hope Valley ghosts and legends 79

The Legend of Robin Hood and Little John of Hathersage 85

Legends of Bradwell and Castleton 89

Edale and the northern moors 98

The High Peak District

Kinder Scout – mermaids, boggarts and white ladies 103

Ghosts and witches of Longdendale 111

The Longdendale Lights 123

Bibliography 128

Introduction

Not many years ago an old lady, who lived in a Derbyshire valley, and had never journeyed beyond her native village, took a delight in telling her grandchildren that the range of crags in Dovedale was the fringe of the world, and that beyond was 'the bad place', the old-fashioned name for Hell. She had, to hear her talk between the whiffs from her long clay pipe (for ladies smoked then), had much experience in a long life of weird warnings. The shepherd dog howled dismally all night on the threshold of the homestead, foretelling the death of Farmer Malkin; and a white cricket leapt across the hearth on the winter's night when Carver's lass strayed off the bridle path on the moor, and was lost in the snow, and frozen to death. The fact that a dog finds sardonic pleasure in howling at night, and that a cricket, like a cat, is prone to jumping, would not have shaken this old lady's faith in these superstitions. But in the cities, in all events, we live in more incredulous days. And now the chances are the howling dog would be kicked off the doorstep, and the cricket if caught would be squashed with an unsentimental boot heel.

'Superstitions of the Peak', in the
Sheffield Daily Telegraph, 14 August 1906

On the present border between the modern counties of Derbyshire and Nottinghamshire, to the south-east of the Peak District National Park, lies a narrow gorge containing dank caves in which evidence of some of the earliest human habitation in Britain has been found. During the last Ice Age, nearly 45,000 years ago, Neanderthal families inhabited the caves of Creswell Crags, near Clowne; and, after the retreat of the glaciers, modern humans arrived at the caves in family groups, hunting horse, reindeer and bison. It is difficult now for us to understand the lifestyle of these early residents of the fringes of what was later to become the Peak District, but there are clues, such as a tiny engraving on a piece of reindeer bone, depicting a figure wearing an animal mask who is perhaps participating in a ritual dance.

The names of the caves at Creswell reflect the rich heritage of folklore and tradition in Derbyshire and the Peak District, which has survived from the mysterious past to the present day. Mother Grundy's Parlour, where the bone carving was discovered, was once the home of a witch, while Robin Hood's Cave nearby is associated with the legendary medieval hero whose name turns up so often in Peakland folklore. The name of Pin Hole Cave refers to the old custom whereby visitors to sacred places used to leave a small offering, in this case a bent pin, to the nature spirits who, even as late as the nineteenth-century, had an important influence upon the lives of countryfolk.

In the Peak District, as in many highland areas of the British Isles, ancient beliefs and traditions live on in the remote hills and valleys. Some anthropologists believe that Celtic peoples may have survived here and absorbed the influx of Romans, Saxons, Danes and Normans.

Prior to the Roman occupation, the northern Peak District was occupied by Celtic tribes, the most powerful of which were the Brigantes: Brigantea being the High One, a goddess of war. The famous 'Shivering Mountain' of Mam Tor – crowned by a hill fort

Mam Tor – the 'Shivering Mountain'

dating from the early Bronze Age – may be named after their mother goddess; while the ram, symbol of the old county of Derbyshire, may symbolise the cult of the horned god, lord of the animals.

The Celtic influence is also reflected in the names of the rivers Derwent, Dove, Dane, Goyt, Rother, Trent, Amber and Noe, which are all of British origin. Celtic place-names, according to Professor Cameron in *The Place-Names of Derbyshire*, cluster in the north-west of the county, where self-sufficient farming communities have lived for 250 generations in the hills of the High Peak, with a minimum amount of interference from the outside world.

Christianity arrived late in the Peak District. Circles of standing stones and windswept barrows litter the hills, standing in silent testimony to a past dominated by the worship of Old Gods. Paganism was a religion closely associated with the everyday life of the people – a worship of nature as embodied in the Earth, the seasons, stones, trees, special places, and above all, water. Many elements of pagan religion – the names and dates of important calendar festivals, the names of gods and goddesses, pilgrimages to holy places and the use of carved images – were taken over and incorporated into a new ideology when the first Christian missionaries arrived in the British Isles.

In the seventh century AD, when Anglo-Saxon warriors and farming families moved north from the midlands into the Peak District, they brought with them fine jewellery and weapons as well as a new form of worship – Christianity. The famous Benty Grange helmet, discovered by Thomas Bateman in the nineteenth century in a barrow on the Ashbourne road south of Buxton, displays a mixture of both pagan and Christian symbols in its metalwork – heralding a time of change. The first recorded mention of the inhabitants of the area occurs in the early Anglo-Saxon 'Tribal Hidage', where the tribe inhabiting the Peak are named as the 'Pecsaetna', or Peak-dwellers, from which the modern name for the region originates.

All over the world, and throughout history, incoming religions brought to a country by missionaries or conquerors have ousted earlier, indigenous, beliefs. But in doing so, invariably the new faith has taken over the shrines of the earlier one, preserving its sites and, often, its structures and associated observances. With the coming of Christianity to the Peak District, the pagan practice of cremating the dead and burying the remains with lavish grave-goods in great earthen barrows ceased, and was replaced by burial in Christian churchyards. But belief in an after-life continued, and the traditions

8

and customs once attached to the pagan barrows were transferred to churchyards, many Peakland churches today having their own ghost story.

The policy of absorbing pagan beliefs into Christianity was necessary, as it took many hundreds of years for the Christian missionaries to make any impression upon believers in the Old Religion, and superstitions rooted in the mysterious pagan past continue in parts of the Peak District today. Every summer, the pretty limestone villages of central Peakland stage the world-famous Well Dressings, which attract thousands of tourists to experience a custom which has survived from a time when water was worshipped for its life-giving properties. Other annual events are the Castleton Garland Day, a curious village festival held in the High Peak district from time immemorial, and the Shrove Tuesday football game held at Ashbourne, which some authorities believe is a survival from ancient times when the game, which resembles a huge rugby scrum, may have been a sacrificial rite to commemorate a battle, with the 'ball' originally being a human head!

The Shrove Tuesday football game at Ashbourne

The study of folklore, customs and traditions helps us to understand the religious beliefs of our ancestors. Examination of different kinds of ritual and superstition, such as animal sacrifice, offerings to earth and water, spells and charms, illustrates patterns of human activity which have continued with little alteration over the centuries.

Past generations of Peak-dwellers firmly believed in the existence of fairies, goblins, giants and a whole menagerie of spirits and omens. The famous legend of the outlaw Little John, who is buried in the churchyard at Hathersage, is only one example of belief in giants. Landscape features were in the past often attributed to their activities; indeed, in the eleventh-century Geoffrey of Monmouth wrote that in Roman times 'the name of the island was Albion, and of none was it inhabited save only of a few giants'. There are caves and crags in Peakland associated with legendary giants, known in some regions as Hob Hurst, a nature spirit whose name is found at Hob Hurst's House, a Bronze Age barrow near Chatsworth House, and Thirst House Cave at Deepdale, near Buxton.

Boggart Lane, Charlesworth, near Glossop

Other places were believed to be haunted by elves and goblins, as at Eldon Hill ('elves' hill') at Peak Forest, Puxhill ('hill of the goblins') at Fernilee, near Whaley Bridge, and at Demon's Dale near Taddington. In local dialect 'boggart' was the name for a troublesome ghost or spirit which today would be described as a poltergeist. There are 'Boggart Stones', 'Boggart Rooms', and even 'Boggart Lanes' surviving today at Charlesworth, near Glossop, and Oughtibridge, on the western outskirts of Sheffield. The name is related to 'barghast', from the German *geist* or spirit, a devilish dog-like creature with 'large saucer-shaped eyes', which terrorised night-travellers on lonely lanes in times gone by.

Many stories describe ghostly black dogs which haunt certain roads, lanes and bridges in the Peakland hills, and indeed throughout the country. In East Anglia the creature is known as 'Black Shuck', whilst in Lancashire and Cumbria it is 'Trash' or 'Skriker'. At Crich, near Matlock, there is Shuckwood and Shuckstonefield, whilst at Hulland, near Duffield in south Derbyshire, there is Shuckton Manor, a house which takes its name from a haunting by a phantom dog. Often places with folklore associations are found close together. At Holmesfield, near Sheffield, are Hob Lane and Bury Hill – a prehistoric mound once the haunt of a ghostly black dog with eyes like saucers which would appear at crossroads as a death omen. At Wirksworth are Hob Hall and Hob Wood, possibly originating from the days when Anglo-Saxon and Scandinavian settlers arrived in the region, populating the hills, mountains and streams with spirits and goblins.

Belief in the existence of ghosts is clearly of ancient origin, before the arrival of street-lighting and good roads spelt the end for the dragons which lurked in the uncharted moors and caverns of Peakland. For in folklore, burial mounds and barrows were populated by spirits of the dead, and contained treasure which was zealously guarded by fearsome serpents. Dragons and serpents survive both in place-names and folklore throughout the region. Wharncliffe Crags, on the edges of the Peak National Park near Sheffield, were once the home of a fearsome fire-breathing dragon which, in a bygone age, ravaged the surrounding countryside and was eventually slain by a Saxon lord, More of More Hall, whose crest displays the dragon symbol. Wormhill, a village near Buxton, has an ancient church dedicated to the dragon-slaying St Margaret, and may take its name from a similar story, now lost, although Knotlow, a conical hill nearby, is said to have been the home of the monster.

In the epic poem *Beowulf,* which some scholars believe was composed for the Mercian royal court in the eighteenth century AD, aerial dragons which today would be reported as Unidentified Flying Objects are described as:

> ... the primeval enemy which haunts the dusk: the scaly, malicious worm which seeks out funeral mounds, and flies burning through the night, wrapped about with flame, to the terror of the countryfolk. Its habit is to seek out treasure buried in the earth, and mount guard over the pagan gold ...

Drakelow ('hill of the dragon'), a prehistoric tumulus near Burton-on-Trent in southern Derbyshire, is mentioned in an Anglo-Saxon charter dating from the year AD772. The dragon's mound is singularly unimpressive today, as it is now covered by a power-station, but in medieval times it was a place of evil repute. In the eleventh century, Galfridus, an abbot of Burton Abbey, recorded that between the years 1083 and 1093 two rebels were executed and buried at Drakelow, but subsequently fearsome spectres appeared and continued to haunt the graves until the bodies were exhumed and burnt. The story ends thus: 'and therefore, the village of Drakelow became forsaken and desolate, and for a long time afterwards none were found so bold as to dwell therein, fearing the judgement of the Lord'.

St Michael was the most powerful archangel in the Christian pantheon, commonly depicted in the act of slaying a dragon or serpent, and was often invoked by Christian missionaries when they came across an area dominated by a strong pagan sun-worshipping cult. The legend of the 'Devil of Drakelow' associates the dragon with a symbol of evil or a manifestation of the Devil, who so often appears in Derbyshire folklore. The famous crooked spire of the parish church in the market town of Chesterfield is described in many folk tales as the work of the Devil, and in the tale of the 'Three Valiant Lads', a number of elements from Peakland folklore are found together. The story, recorded by the scholar Ruth Tongue in *Forgotten Folk Tales,* concerns Winlatter Rock, on East Moor, between Baslow and Chesterfield. The rock does not exist today, but a cave on Birchen Edge, off the moorland road between Baslow and Chesterfield, is known as Wormstall or 'dragon's den', a place avoided in the past. In the story the dragon was a personification of the Devil, who came out of the north and laid waste to all the land, but he was challenged by a priest who climbed Winlatter Rock and held out his arms in the form of a cross, his feet sinking deep into the earth. On a second visit, the

Chesterfield Church – famous for its crooked spire

dragon visited Chesterfield and devastated the land, but was again challenged, this time by three young brothers, who fashioned a huge iron sword which they erected on Winlatter Rock. As the dragon approached, raising a great tempest, the lads gathered the men of Chesterfield and the church bells rang, with lightning flashing from the sword on the rock. This overcame the power of the dragon, who disappeared down Blue John Cave at Castleton, never to be seen again!

Fantastic stories of ghosts and dragons are not confined to the distant past, but are present today in the most unexpected of places. In September 1987 the *Sheffield Star* carried a front-page news story entitled 'Ghost Sightings on New Road', which described a series of strange happenings on the Stocksbridge by-pass road then under construction, in the north-east of the Peak National Park:

> Terrified security guards called in police and clergymen after spotting 'ghosts' on a by-pass being built near Sheffield. A sergeant and police constable sent to the scene – near Stocksbridge – later said they 'felt a presence' as they patrolled . . . but South Yorkshire police have refused to comment on the incident, or on reports that the panda car was jolted by mysterious thuds.

These stories are typical of the rich tapestry of folklore and human experience which provides the material in our survey of the ghosts and legends of the Peak District. This book should be used as a mysteriography – a geography book of the supernatural landscape – placing on record odd happenings, mysteries, ancient lore and traditions which are rapidly dying out, but still sought by visitors to the Peak District. Tastes have changed since the eighteenth century, when Daniel Defoe described it as a 'howling wilderness . . . the most desolate, wild and abandoned country in all England'.

Today, every year tourists wander around the famous grave of Little John in the churchyard at Hathersage, and wonder at the huge mute slabs of stone and earthen banks which make up the great henge and stone circle at Arbor Low. These are reminders of a distant past when the presence of restive spirits, nature gods and fearsome dragons was an everyday fact of life. Whether we believe or not, in the end we are left only with mystery, an ingredient which is necessary in all our lives. 'Mystery', said the astronaut Neil Armstrong in 1969, 'creates wonder, and wonder is the basis for man's desire to understand. Who knows what mysteries will be solved in our lifetime, and what new riddles will become the challenge of the new generations?'

14

Central Peakland

Ghosts and legends of central Peakland

Many ghost stories are told in the villages which cluster on the central plateau of Peakland between the Hope and Wye valleys, especially in the region around Eyam, where the limestone geology slowly gives way to gritstone in the north, a change reflected in the make-up of the drystone walls which are such a distinctive feature of the undulating landscape. Shady Lane, which links the quaint villages of Ashford-in-the-Water and Great Longstone, north-east of Bakewell, is the scene of the appearance of a macabre procession of twelve headless men who carry an empty coffin. According to Clarence Daniel, Shady Lane is avoided by the older generation of locals at dusk and dawn, for it is said that to see the phantom funeral is a forewarning of death.

Another unpleasant ghost appears in the vicinity of the 300-year-old Eyre Arms public house in the village of Hassop. Here the haunting is by a ghostly cavalier who materialises in front of customers and passing motorists, one of whom is reputed to have been killed after swerving to avoid a coach and horses crossing his path. Nearby Hassop Hall, the residence of the Earl of Newburgh, is also said to be haunted, and its grounds once contained a prophetic beech tree which is said to have pronounced upon the rightful ownership of the hall. At one time the ownership of the Hassop estates was a matter of great dispute and the story goes that 'when the wind is exactly in the west, the rustling of the tree distinctly murmurs "All hail, true heir, that stills my voice!"'; some say the words are 'All hail the Eyre that stills my voice!' Local lore adds that many attempts were made over the years to chop down the tree by the owners 'but no sooner has the axe been taken up than some accident happens to the would-be destroyer'.

Other trees were regarded as sacred by Peak-dwellers in the past, and in folklore the Druids – the pagan priests of the Celts – are said to have worshipped in forests and sacred groves, the word Druid meaning 'knowing the oak'. Robin Hood is also associated with the greenwood, with another sacred tree: the venerable Major Oak in

Sherwood Forest being one of his alleged hideouts; a lesser-known Robin Hood's Oak once stood on the precipitous Wharncliffe Crags, north of Sheffield, just outside the boundaries of the Peak District.

The most famous oak in Derbyshire was the Mandrake Tree, also known as the Haunted Oak, which once stood in the grounds of The Hagge (now a farmhouse) at Nether Handley, near Staveley. It is recorded that the tree dated from the reign of Henry VIII, and was flourishing until the nineteenth century, when it was uprooted and destroyed during a great storm in 1883. This ancient oak was venerated by the local population, who believed that it would shriek and bleed if anyone was to cut a bough from it; it also had the reputation of being the only tree in the region which bore mistletoe – sacred to the Druids. It was believed that the strange tree was haunted by a fearsome ghost, one of the many forest spirits which played an important role in country life.

In Derbyshire folklore the rowan or mountain ash had magical powers against witchcraft and the evil eye, a belief that dates back to the Anglo-Saxons, if not earlier; rowan twigs were placed across butter-tubs, and the tubs themselves were sometimes made from the wood of the rowan as a precaution against bewitchment. Sprigs of rowan are still used by people in the village of Bradfield, near Sheffield, as talismans to promote good luck. Similarly, sacred yew trees were often planted in churchyards as a protection against evil and as a symbol of everlasting life. There are many ancient yews to be found in the Peak District, such as the famous Darley Yew, and lesser-known examples such as the half-dead specimen in the grounds of Thryft House Farm at Ringinglow, near Hathersage. This is twenty-five feet tall and according to some authorities could be between 350 and 2,520 years in age. Like other ancient trees, it is thought to have been used as a boundary marker in the medieval period.

The earliest settlements in the dry limestone plateau region of Peakland were usually near rivers, springs and wells. These life-giving sources of water were so important to the everyday life of the pastoral farmers that they took on magical properties in folklore and legend. Springs and wells were thought to be protected by spirits and gods, who were appeased by offerings of flowers and greenery. The mystical importance of water and water sources no doubt soon came to the attention of the first Christian missionaries, who encountered great difficulties when they tried to prevent the worship of wells and springs. In the seventh century Theodore, Archbishop of Canterbury, in his *Capitula,* decreed that 'no one shall go to trees, or wells, or stones, or enclosures, or anywhere else except to God's church, and there make vows or release himself from them'. Later, in the Canons of King Edgar in the tenth century, there is the following plea: 'We enjoin that every priest to zealously promote Christianity and totally extinguish every heathenism; and forbid well-worshipping and necromancies, and divinations, and worship . . . with various trees and stones'.

Despite these prohibitions, worship of nature continued in the countryside, and water-worship has survived to the present in Peakland under the auspices of the Christian Church, in the form of the famous annual Well Dressings. These are spread between late May and early September, so as to fit in with Christian festivals such as Ascension Day, and more recently with Bank Holidays. One of the earliest dressings in the year is at Tissington, a village which has enjoyed a continuous supply from its water sources since 1615, when a severe drought was experienced. The first modern record of well-dressing in the region dates from the year 1758, when Nicholas Hardinge described how he had seen, at the village of Tissington, 'springs adorned with garlands . . . in honour of these fountains, which . . . are annually commemorated on Holy Thursday'.

Well Dressings are very elaborate occasions today, but originally the water sources would have been adorned with simple garlands of flowers and greenery. Most probably the custom dates back to the pagan Celtic period, when offerings were made to water gods. The early Christian missionaries handled pagan customs sensitively, absorbing and adapting rather than suppressing – for instance dedicating holy wells to Christian saints. On the southern edge of the Peak District is the twelfth-century church of St Oswald, at Ashbourne in Derbyshire. The church guide notes how 'the Christian missionaries often founded their churches on pagan religious sites including "holy" wells and this may have happened here, as water of considerable depth contained in a well-like shape has been divined within the centre of the tower.'

Pagan 'magic' was often skilfully tolerated under a veneer of Christianity, with the names of important calendar festivals and pagan gods converted to the use of the new religion. The goddess Brigid, associated with many holy wells, became the Christian St Brigid; similarly, Anu (a mother goddess) became St Ann – whose well is the centre of the Buxton water-cult – and the Celtic water sprite Elen became St Helen.

A Peak District well dressing

For many hundreds of years, lead and other minerals have been mined in the Peak District and the industry has left an enduring imprint upon the landscape and its inhabitants. In the limestone regions lead has been extracted since Roman times, when ingots from a place known as 'Lutudarum', which has never been identified on the ground, were an important economic resource. In the eighteenth and nineteenth century much lead-mining took place on a smaller scale, with mines run by small groups of local workers whose customs and beliefs live on in folklore.

In 1938 G. L. Hayto wrote in *Derbyshire Countryside* of the many superstitions once held by miners in the region. 'Reference can still be found', he noted, 'to a ghostly dog which prowled around old mines and soughs and was considered an ill omen'. A story from Bradwell, near Castleton, tells how a miner returning home from a game of cards was terrified by the sudden appearance in the moonlight of 'a strange and perfectly black dog of unusual size, that came slowly up to them and vanished under their feet'. Despite repeatedly calling the attention of his companion to the apparition, the miner was unable to convince him that there was anything to be seen:

> . . . the other, however, was so assured of the vision being a judgement and an omen of evil, that he refrained himself, and sought in vain to prevent his fellow worker from going down the mine on the following day. The latter, however, went and perished, the roof of the mine falling upon him.

Another unexplained phantom of the mines was the 'knocker', a weird noise sometimes heard by miners close at hand and sometimes deep down in the earth, which some said would lead, if followed, to the discovery of new ores. The knockers were often associated with fairies, and lights seen in mines and above certain stretches of ground were taken as a sure indication of the presence of rich mineral veins. In Castleton and other areas of the Peak the appearance of 'the Fiery Drake', a strange ball of flame, was believed to indicate the presence of lead ore in the direction it pointed – this superstition held good for many centuries and is mentioned in many old mining manuals. In other cases the appearance of lights in old mine-shafts was believed to be an omen of death.

A number of mines in the Peak are haunted; most notable of these is the Magpie Mine, a deep disused shaft now run as a field centre by the Peak District Mines Historical Society. The mine, south of the village of Sheldon, near Bakewell, has some of the best preserved lead-mining buildings in the area. Magpie Mine was worked for three hundred years until its closure in 1924, and it is said that there is a curse on the workings as they have been continually afflicted with floods, fires and falls. The curse may originate from the year 1833, when three men were suffocated in the lead workings, and today the place retains an eerie atmosphere.

In 1946 a party of explorers in the mine reported seeing, and photographing, a ghost. R. A. H. O'Neil describes how:

> . . . one of them reported that he had seen a man with a candle walking along a tunnel from which he had disappeared without trace. A photograph of another member of the party on a raft in a sough at the mine showed a second man standing, apparently, on nine feet of water. The Old Man was clearly either trying to protect his ancient rights or to help the twentieth-century searchers find the ore, which is reported to be thick and pure in the main vein now 150 feet below the water level.

Another ghost haunts Sallet Hole Mine, near Stoney Middleton, where a figure wearing a long coat and cap has been spotted in the workings, who vanishes into thin air; while at Hanging Flatt Mine, near Eyam, appears a ghost known as 'th' owd mon'. He wanders around the old fluorspar workings with a spade over his shoulder, muttering to himself, seemingly oblivious to those who hear his phantom footsteps. One lady who lived in a farm overlooking the mine told Clarence Daniel that she had heard 'the strokes of a pick within the mine although it was actually closed at the time'.

Bakewell and district

The town of Bakewell is today the natural 'capital' of the Peak District, and certainly the largest town in the Peak National Park. A centre of the tourist industry, it attracts thousands of visitors each year, who come in search of the famous local delicacy, the 'Bakewell Pudding' (a sticky tart), and to attend the annual Bakewell Show. The Show is a focal point in the calendar of the Peakland farming community, and continues the attraction of the town as a market centre, the right to hold a Monday market being granted in the year 1330.

The name of the town was first recorded in the tenth century as 'Badecan wiellon', meaning 'Beadeca's spring', presumably a reference to the tepid iron-bearing springs which once made Bakewell a spa, though never a competitor of Buxton. There are many traces of prehistoric man in the region, especially on the high ground to the north-east of the town, the site of an Iron Age hill fort at Ball Cross. The fort when excavated yielded pottery, a quernstone and a cup-and-ring marked (see page 44) boulder. Another ancient site was Heathenslow, the name of a barrow recorded in the thirteenth century, whose location is now lost.

The first written reference to Bakewell occurs in the Anglo-Saxon Chronicle, where in an entry under the year AD924 it is recorded that 'before mid summer, King Edward [the Elder] went with his force to Nottingham . . . then he went thence into Peakland, to Bakewell, and commanded a castle to be built nigh there unto, and garrisoned.'

The castle referred to no longer exists, and its location is a mystery, although there are defensive earthworks north-east of the town, where a mound known as Castle Hill stands on a natural eminence above a medieval bridge over the River Wye. In the grounds of the 'castle', which is thought to date from the time of King Stephen, is Lady Manners School. One corridor in the boarding school is said to be haunted by the ghost of Jim Marlowe, a former butler who shot himself in the pantry. His ghost is said to haunt the corridor leading to the gun-room, along which unexplained footsteps have been heard on patrol.

Menacing gargoyles in the church porch at Bakewell

In the Domesday Book it is recorded that there were two priests at the church in Bakewell, a testimony to the early importance of the town. The impressive hilltop church of All Saints contains a fascinating collection of carved stones of Anglo-Saxon and Norman origin, including fragments of gravestones, carved crosses and other decorated stones salvaged from the surroundings. Dr Cox, in his book on the churches of Derbyshire, stated that the collection of carved stones was 'without rival either in number or variety' elsewhere. The original Saxon church was replaced by a new structure in the twelfth century, but much stone remains from the older building which was probably the focus of an important early Christian community, perhaps a monastic centre in the Anglo-Saxon kingdom of Mercia. In addition to the fine gargoyles and carved heads on the outside of the church, inside the chancel contains finely carved wooden misericords depicting fantastic monsters including a dragon with a human head, grotesque winged creatures, a mermaid and a 'Green Man', from whose grinning mouth sprouts a wreath of foliage.

In the churchyard are two Saxon crosses, one of which was unearthed in a field at Darley Dale. Outside the Vernon Chapel stands a fine carved preaching cross, eight feet in height, and dating from the eighth century. The carvings on the cross are much eroded but depict scenes from the Bible as well as images from pagan mythology, including the gods Odin and Loki. The cross, in fact, once stood at the crossroads one mile to the south of the nearby village of Hassop, a spot connected with a legend dating from the sixteenth century. It was then that the Prince of Wales, Prince Arthur, the son of Henry VII, was a frequent visitor to nearby Haddon Hall, then the home of his governor, Sir Henry Vernon.

One evening in September 1501, so the story goes, the Prince, after spending a day wandering along the banks of the Wye, rested at the foot of the Great Cross at Hassop. As he dozed a strange vision materialised: '. . . a tall thin female dressed in white; her features sunken and wan, her lips of an ashy hue, and her eyeballs protruding, bright and motionless'. The vision warned him of his impending fate:

Unhappy royal Prince, mourn not that fate which is not thine! One earthly pageant awaits thee, yea, it is at hand; and then, ah! then, thou wilt drop into the lap of thy mother – thy mother earth! Forth comes to Britain's shore thy lovely, smiling bride – ah! ah! bride and widow of a royal boy!

22

Haddon Hall, near Bakewell

The prophetic vision was soon to come true to the word, as when the Prince returned to Haddon Hall that evening he was greeted with the news that his Spanish bride-to-be had arrived in England and he was to be married without delay. After only four months, however, the Prince succumbed to illness and died just as the vision had foretold, his last words being, 'O, the vision of the cross at Haddon!'

In 1607 Bakewell was the scene of the execution for witchcraft of two sisters, the owners of a milliner's business and boarding house, who were the victims of bizarre accusations involving supernatural teleportation. The case is unusual in the annals of witch-hunting, in that the alleged witches were not accused of murder or any other malevolent act; rather they were incriminated on the evidence of a Scotsman who had been lodging in the house of Mrs Stafford, one of the sisters. He had witnessed them chanting a spell, on repeating which he found himself whisked away through the air and deposited in a cellar in London, where he was arrested on suspicion of intended robbery. His improbable story was enough in those days to convict the 'Derbyshire Witches', who were executed shortly afterwards, their deaths bemoaned by the historian Stephen Glover who wrote that 'nor is it a wonder that innocence should suffer under that weak and witch-ridden monarch, James I'.

Ghosts and spectres of the 'Plague Village'

The present church of St Lawrence at Eyam is believed to date from the reign of Henry I, although it is said that an earlier church stood on the site in Saxon times. The church was originally dedicated to St Helen, in Christian mythology the mother of the first Christian Roman Emperor, Constantine, and the finder of the true Cross. Like many other Christian saints, it is thought that St Helen replaced a pagan deity, possibly the Celtic Elen, often connected with holy wells and Roman roads. The church's connection with the saint or goddess is supported by a medieval condition of tenure, which required the Stafford family to 'maintain one lamp burning before the altar of St Helen' whenever Divine Service was taking place at the altar. A stone cross known as St Helen's Cross, now fixed to the north wall, is thought by some to have been where the original lamp of St Helen stood.

Eyam plague cottage

Eyam is of course famous as the village whose water supply became so important during the attack of the Great Plague in 1665–6. The epic sacrifice made by the rector, William Mompesson, whose wife Catherine died at the height of the outbreak, in his efforts to isolate the village from the surrounding countryside in order to stop the spread of the disease, has passed into legend. The three wells which are dressed at Eyam on the last Saturday in August every year are some of the best attended in the Peak District and have a special poignancy, with scenes on the well picture-boards often commemorating the Eyam Plague, in which over three hundred of the population died. On Sir William Hill, one mile outside the village, lies Mompesson's Well, a spring where food was left for the villagers by the people outside; there are other sad reminders of the plague victims at other spots around the village.

The late Clarence Daniel, author of two books on Derbyshire ghosts, lived in Eyam and collected stories of many local hauntings and their associated folklore. One of the hauntings concerned the supposed ghost of Catherine Mompesson, who is said to appear in the rectory at Eyam, the scene of her death from the plague of 1665–6. A former maid at the rectory told how she had seen her ghost walking up the back stairs wearing a large hat! Other strange happenings include phantom footsteps in the night, as well as doors opening and closing.

Eyam Dale is the scene of a weird haunting by a 'phantom cyclist', who has apparently been spotted by many locals at night in the vicinity of Top Scrin, at the top of the dale. The ghost is sometimes heard but not seen, and on other occasions has been sighted in the pouring rain, but without a spot of moisture trickling from his cape as he hurtles past the astonished onlooker. The Tudor-style Eyam Hall was haunted by a ghostly white horse, as well as the wraith of an old man who appeared at one time in a top-storey room, which resulted in the room always being kept locked.

In the village itself, the Miner's Arms public house, which dates to the year 1630, was once the meeting-place of the Barmote Court which legislated over the local mining industry. The plaque above the door tells how the old inn 'is reputed to be one of the most haunted in the village and has seen many strange events'; certain rooms in the building are said to have an eerie 'atmosphere', and several landlords have told of feeling a ghostly presence. A former parish council chairman reported seeing an elderly lady dressed in boots, black bonnet and sequin-trimmed cape entering the pub after its

Eyam Hall, haunted by an old man and a white horse

The Miner's Arms, Eyam, 'one of the most haunted houses in the village'

restoration; it was thought probable that this may have been the wife of a former landlord, who was murdered in the seventeenth century.

Another haunted pub is the Derwentwater Arms at nearby Calver, where a room has a reputation for being haunted, and is avoided by guests. The ghost is thought to be that of a former landlord, who had a penchant for playing practical jokes on his customers. One day he pretended to be dead, only to sit up and frighten them, covered in a white sheet. The very next day, however, the landlord received his come-uppance, as he fell from his horse-drawn trap on the way home from Bakewell and was killed!

A secluded wooded valley known as Bretton Clough divides the two heather-covered uplands of Eyam Moor and Offerton Moor, across the valley from Calver. It is an ancient place, with a Celtic name meaning 'the farm of the Britons'. The clough has an eerie reputation in the neighbouring villages, for it was said at one time that it was haunted by a 'phantom huntsman and hounds'. In *The Ghost Book,* A. A. McGregor writes that among the people who claim to have seen the phantom huntsman were the Revd Brooksbank, a former vicar of Hathersage Church, and the Hodgkinson sisters, owners of Moorseats Hall. Dr Mary Andrews, of Shatton, the author of *Long*

Eerie Bretton Clough – abode of a phantom huntsman and hounds

Ago in Peakland also reports that during the 1930s she and a companion heard in the clough 'a hunting horn, for which she could find no explanation. Not for years thereafter was she to learn for the first time of the phantom huntsfolk and their phantom hounds'.

Belief in a phantom huntsman is of very ancient origin, for Germanic mythology tells of the 'Wild Hunt', a pack of spectral hounds who glide through the air on stormy nights led by a figure on a white horse. Often this phantom aerial hunt was heard and not seen, the distinctive noises entering folklore as the Gabriel Hounds or Gabble Ratchets. The belief in the reality of these uncanny noises was at one time very strong throughout the Peak District, and the appearance of the Gabriel Hounds was supposed to be a sure sign that death would soon visit the neighbourhood. As late as the 1870s, when a Sheffield child was killed in a fire, the neighbours immediately called to mind how the Gabriel Hounds had passed above the house not long before.

The famous 'Celtic cross' now standing in the churchyard at Eyam originally came from a site on the moors above the village, where it may have acted as a preaching centre when Christianity first arrived in the valley. The cross is of Anglo-Saxon origin, with Celtic and Norse influence in the carving style resulting in a mixture of pagan and Christian symbolism. There are depictions of the Madonna and child as well as interlacing runic designs of Scandinavian origin. The cross may have originally stood on Eyam Moor, where the centre of prehistoric religion in the region was the Bronze Age stone circle known as Wet Withens.

All that remains of the circle today is a low earthen bank with ten small standing stones, which are easy to miss in the heather. From the circle, the visitor can obtain one of the most beautiful views in the Peak District, with the gritstone edges and heather-covered moors stretching out to the north-eastern horizon. Dr John Barnatt discovered that the circle is aligned on the midsummer sunrise, which took place when he was standing in the circle, above the flat-topped rock outcrop of Higgar Tor on the moors north-east of Hathersage. Higgar Tor, which stands adjacent to a defended earthwork known as Carl Wark on Hathersage Moor, is an impressive rock escarpment named after Odin, the Norse god, and is thought to have been an area sacred in prehistory. John Barnatt concluded that Wet Withens had been carefully placed so as to take maximum advantage of the landscape features for astronomical observation by prehistoric man.

Baslow Edge – a distinctive gritstone 'edge' in eastern Peakland

Ancient beliefs linked to stone circles, standing stones and natural outcrops of rock have survived in the Peak District and other upland areas from prehistory into the twentieth century, often living on only in folklore and legend. On Baslow Edge, near Wellington's Monument, is a large isolated block of stone, much eroded by the elements, known as the Eagle Stone. The name may be from Egglestone, or 'witches' stone', and folklore tells how the girls of Baslow would resist any proposal of marriage until the man had shown his prowess by scaling the stone, and thus gaining favour with the witches. Another theory is that the rock is named after the pagan god Aigle, a giant who was capable of throwing huge stones.

The Eagle Stone, like the Mother's Cap on Over Owler Tor near Hathersage, was regarded as sacred in prehistoric times and it is possible that some of these stones were used as markers for astronomical alignments, due to their prominence on the skyline. The use of stones in this manner may be preserved in folklore, which tells how the Eagle Stone 'is said to turn around at cock-crow'. The same legend is attached to other outcrops of rock, including the Turning Stone, near Ashover, and the Head Stone or Stump John, which stands on the Hallam Moors near Sheffield. This stone is a conspicuous object in the landscape, standing over twenty feet in height, and is said to 'turn around on a certain morning in the year when it hears the cock-crow'. In recent years the folklore surrounding the Head Stone has been investigated more closely, when several visitors noted that at certain times of the year, especially in late August, a distinctive human 'face' can be seen clearly when the sun shines on the west side of the stone. Other stones were thought to have powers over human fertility and even be able to grant wishes. A lump of rock known as the Wishing Stone, at Lumsdale on the hillside above Matlock, is said to have the power of granting a wish to those who walk around it three times. Another similar wishing stone once existed in Faybrick wood, near Ashover, and it was said that if you sat upon it and wished three times your wish would be granted. There are many similar beliefs attached to standing stones, which may relate to the days when stones were worshipped, like the trees and wells already mentioned, as the homes of nature spirits. Fairies were believed to dance around standing stones and barrows, and at Calver it was once said that the little people could be seen in the dusk of evening, dancing in a certain meadow called the 'Stocking Field'.

The Eagle Stone, said to 'turn around at cock-crow'

Tideswell and district

A ceremony known as church-clypping was once held at the village of Tideswell, where the congregation would join with others from Litton and Miller's Dale to encircle the church, holdings hands whilst singing 'We love the place O God, wherein thine honour dwells'. It has been suggested that church-clypping, which still takes place every year at Wirksworth and Burbage, near Buxton, may be the remains of an ancient dancing rite once practised at a standing stone or circle which previously stood on the site of the church. Clarence Daniel wrote in *Derbyshire Customs* that the great medieval church at Tideswell was formerly encircled 'with stone crosses set up at points where parishioners from outlying parts might catch their first glimpse of the pinnacles of the ancient "Cathedral of the Peak"'.

Tideswell takes its name either from one of the numerous wells that once existed in the village, or from a Saxon who may be buried at Tideslow ('Tidi's burial mound') nearby. In the Domesday survey Tideswell was a chapelry in the extensive parish of Hope, and the first reference to a church occurs in the twelfth century. The dedication to St John the Baptist may have been in deference to the past importance of the village as a centre of water-worship, for the 'Ebbing and Flowing Well', now lying in a rockery on Manchester Road, was once rated as one of the 'Seven Wonders of the Peak'. The modern revival of well-dressing in Tideswell began in the 1820s, when two springs in a garden on Sherwood Road began to be dressed regularly.

In 1824 Ebenezer Rhodes wrote that the oldest place of worship in Tideswell was in fact a stone chapel or oratory, constructed in the reign of King John, well before the present church was built. The chapel stood on the road into the town from Stoney Middleton and it was said to be connected with the chancel of the new church by an underground passage. 'From this place', he wrote, 'unseen choristers were sometimes distinctly heard hymning the sweetest strains, as they seemed to pass in slow procession along the vaulted passages [towards] the church, where the sounds seemed to die away.' This ghostly procession was said to indicate the approaching death of the more important inhabitants of the village. The old chapel was demolished, however, many years before Rhodes' description, and it is said that when it was unfloored many human bones were found within it.

The eighteenth-century George Hotel in the village is haunted by a ghost known as 'Old Sarah', a woman around fifty-five years old and dressed like a serving wench in a long Victorian dress and cap. Local legend says her ghost haunts the pub late at night in search of her lost husband; her apparition in the 1930s is supposed to have scared away a party of guests. When a new landlord moved into the hotel in 1980, his father saw the ghost appear in the bar, where he had been sleeping on the sofa, late one night. The landlord Dale Norris said afterwards that 'my father didn't mention anything until two or three nights later. Then one night a customer asked us if we had seen anything yet. My father then said he had seen the ghost.'

Near Tideswell is Wheston Hall, originally of seventeenth century date, and once the proud residence of John Shaw, a Steward of the High Peak Courts, when it was a three-storey mansion dominating the tiny hamlet. Since that time the hall has been restructured, but still retains its ghostly reputation. Over four separate ghosts are supposed to haunt the building, including the 'Old Woman of Wheston Hall', wearing a crinoline dress and bonnet, and the spectre of another lady who 'passes three times round the house, barefooted in her nightgown, shrieking and tearing her golden hair'. The story goes that this ghost is that of a woman from Tideswell, who was forced to marry a man she did not love; her intended lover moved to Wheston Hall and lived a solitary existence, practising, it was rumoured locally, black magic. Eventually, the two lovers conspired to murder the woman's husband, and it is said his body is buried in the orchard. The lady's ghost thereafter was said to leave her grave in Tideswell to visit the scene of the murder in the orchard. Another version places the murder in the cellar, where immovable bloodstains are reported to appear.

Another ghost of Wheston Hall was known as 'Soldier Dick', and his story resembles that of the guardian skull at Tunstead Farm (see page 70), several miles away. Soldier Dick was a life-size model soldier dressed in Cromwellian armour which stood for many years in the reception hall of the building. It was said that if the model was moved from its accustomed place, misfortunes would soon follow, with ill-health affecting the owners themselves, as well as crop failure and cattle disease plaguing the farm. However, if treated with respect, Soldier Dick acted as a guardian of the interests of the farm and its owners. The ghost was 'laid' however, when the hall was renovated, as the model was buried in the cellar under tons of rubble!

More tales of violent death are told at the hamlet of Wardlow Miers, between Tideswell and Eyam, on the A623 road – the scene on New Year's Day, 1815, of the brutal murder of a toll-bar keeper, Hannah Oliver, by Anthony Lingard, a twenty-one-year old man from

Tideswell. He was caught and convicted of the crime and duly executed; his body, as was the custom in those days as a warning to others, was hung in chains from a gibbet on Peter's Stone, an isolated outcrop of limestone which stands in a deep wooded gorge between Wardlow and Litton. The gruesome memory of the murder and execution has no doubt contributed to the belief that the area is haunted, and more than one cyclist has reported the sensation of being strangled by invisible hands whilst resting at the wayside in Wardlow Miers.

Hob Hurst and Demon's Dale

Wardlow lies to the north of Monsal Dale, mentioned in the fifteenth century by William of Worcester, in his *Itinarium*. Here a valley was known from ancient times as Dimin or Demon's Dale, part of the gorge formed by the River Wye in the parish of Taddington. Worcester clearly interpreted the name as meaning the 'demon's valley', when he wrote that 'the River Wye runs by the town of Marnsdale (Monsal Dale), a valley called Dymynsdale, where spirits are tortured, which is a marvellous entrance into the land of the Peke, where souls are tormented . . .'

Monsal Dale and the gorge of the River Wye

Monsal Dale is today one of the Peak District's busiest tourist attractions, with visitors flocking to the stunning scenic valley, crossed by the famous five-arched railway viaduct opened in 1863 to carry the London-Midland line. This act of progress was attacked by the artist John Ruskin, who despised how the railway line had 'blasted its rocks away, heaped thousands of rocks into its lovely stream. The valley is gone and the Gods with it, and now every fool in Buxton can be at Bakewell in half an hour and every fool in Bakewell at Buxton; which you think a lucrative process of exchange – you Fools everywhere.' In a much-quoted appreciation of Monsal Dale, Ruskin described it as:

> ... a rocky valley between Buxton and Bakewell, once upon a time as divine as the Vale of Tempe; you might have seen the Gods there morning and evening – Apollo and all the sweet muses of the light – walking in fair procession on the lawns of it, and to and fro among the pinnacles of its crags.

Ruskin was probably aware of the legend of Hulac Warren and Hedessa, a mythological saga connected with the region from time immemorial. Lying half-submerged in an elbow of a bend in the River Wye, close to the A6 Bakewell to Buxton road, is the Warren Stone, a weathered limestone crag which, according to legend, is the petrified remains of the leader of a race of giants who once lived in the recesses of Demon's Dale. The giant was Hulac Warren (Hector Warren in some versions of the story), who was turned to stone by the gods as a punishment for attempting to rape a beautiful shepherdess, Hedessa. The legend was enshrined in verse by Eliza Blore in 1816, who wrote:

> *Beneath the Hough where transverse valleys meet,*
> *Is Demon's Dale, a dreary lone retreat –*
> *Need I relate (what neighbouring peasants say),*
> *How Hulac Warren here concealed lay,*
> *Surprised and carried to this horrid den,*
> *The fairest daughter of the sons of men ...*

The verse describes how Hedessa resisted Warren's advances, and in the process fell, or threw herself, to her death from 'the peak of yon cavernous tors'. Near the place where she fell 'a stream of pure water, pure as her own soul, gushed forth into being; and while these mountains, and these woods and valleys remain, the spirit of Hedessa will visit these scenes, and bless with its presence the flowing water of the Hedess Spring ...':

Hence rose the Hedess Spring.
Hulac blasphemed the Gods and to atone
The heinous crime was turned to Warren Stone.

The age of this legend is difficult to determine, but its core may be of pagan Celtic origin, and a version of it may have once been told by the inhabitants of the Iron Age fort known as Finn Cop, whose ramparts tower 1,072 feet above the valley of the Wye, commanding a dramatic viewpoint across a landscape of limestone crags, tumbling streams and wooded slopes. A local rhyme runs:

The piper of Shacklow,
The fiddler of Finn,
The old woman of Demon's Dale,
Calls them all in.

This describes places in the valley of legendary significance, Shacklow being a wood close to the entrance to the valley. Nearby was a field at the lower opening of the gorge on which it was said witches would dance at night. The fiddler referred to is the giant Hulac or Hob, whose abode was across the valley from Finn Cop at Hob's House, otherwise known as Hob Thirst Hole. Hob's House is a mass of tumbled limestone rocks, rented by dark fissures and cracks. A human skeleton of early British date was discovered in a cave here, and the name Hob Thirst (Hob Hurst) can be translated literally as 'giant's house', 'hurst' being an old English name for a wood or forest. Ebenezer Rhodes, in his *Peak Scenery* (1824), says that there was a tradition then existing that the cave:

> . . . was inhabited by a being of gigantic stature, who was possessed of great and mysterious powers, and who was known by the name of Hob. This extraordinary personage never appeared by day; but when the inhabitants were asleep in their beds, he traversed the vales, entered their houses, thrashed their corn, and in one single night did the work of ten day labourers, unseen and unheard, for which service he was recompensed with a bowl of cream, that was duly placed upon the hearth, to be quaffed on the completion of the task.

Hob Hurst is a name found frequently in folklore, where he appears as a wood elf or fairy, the equivalent of Puck or Robin Goodfellow. Many traditions concerning this being existed in remote Derbyshire villages until the Victorian age; he was believed to inhabit stone circles, barrows and other lonely places, and so strong was the belief in him that in some areas people would not venture near his abodes at certain hours for fear of harm. When in good humour, Hob made everything on the farm, especially in the dairy, go smoothly and prosperously: the cows give plenty of milk, the cream churned quickly into butter, and the quantity of hay was increased. However, when irritated he would make the cows go dry, the milk turn sour, the crockery smash, and would generally upset the harmony of man's relationship with nature. In the past, to avoid such misfortune, a bowl of cream was left for Hob on the hearth of many Derbyshire homes, as well as at certain sacred places, as an offering to the pagan god of the fields and fertility at key dates in the farming calendar.

Other Hob Hurst's Houses are to be found in the same region. In Deepdale, a limestone gorge south of King Sterndale near Buxton, there is a rock cavern known as Thirst House Cave, written 'Tursthous' in 1417, which is translated as 'giant's house'. Many prehistoric and Roman remains have been discovered in this cave, which was near a spring where local people used to go on an annual pilgrimage, for its waters were believed to be charmed or blessed by the goblin which inhabited the cave. It was said that people who drank from the spring on Good Friday morning were healed of their complaints, a clear survival of a pagan belief. Another cave, also named Hob Hurst's House, where once again prehistoric remains including a complete skeleton as well as flint arrowheads, bronze brooches and an iron adze (cutting tool) have been discovered, is Thor's Cave, above the River Dove in the Manifold Valley, in northern Staffordshire. The cave, and the nearby village of Wetton, are named after Thor, the Norse god of thunder, and his father Woden. The cave and others in the same locality are said to be the haunts of spirits and fairies, including 'Fiddling Hob Hurst', whose screeching has been heard by those sensitive to such things.

Hob Hurst was also associated with prehistoric burial mounds, which in the past were the dwelling places of spirits. Not far from Chatsworth House, near the remains of a stone circle at Park Gate, is a Bronze Age burial mound known as Hob Hurst House. It consists of a high circular mound of earth, thirty-two feet in diameter. It was excavated in 1853 by Thomas Bateman who discovered a circular stone-lined cist containing cremated human bones 'lying in the very spot where they had been drawn together while the embers of the funeral pyre were glowing'. He wrote:

. . . in the popular name given to the barrow, we have an indirect testimony to its great antiquity, as Hobhurst's House signifies the abode of an unearthly or supernatural being, accustomed to haunt woods and other solitary places, respecting whom many traditions linger in remote villages. Such an idea could only arise in a superstitious age long ago . . . it likewise affords a curious instance of the inherent tendency of the mind to assign a reason for everything uncommon or unaccountable, which no extent of ignorance or apathy seems able totally to eradicate.

The White Peak

Ghosts and legends of the White Peak

The village of Youlgreave stands on a hill above the River Bradford, once a prosperous market town and centre of the local lead-mining industry. The earliest record of a church at Youlgreave is from 1152, when the squire of the village – a descendent of the Saxon lord mentioned in the Domesday Book – made a gift of the church and its dependent chapels of Elton, Winster, Stanton, Middleton and Gratton to the Abbey of St Mary at Leicester. The present medieval church is one of the oldest and largest of its kind in Peakland, and probably stands on the site of an earlier Saxon structure.

South of the village is the Long Rake, a mineral vein which runs between Youlgreave and the nearby stone circle of Arbor Low. Wenley Hill has old fluorspar mines, and is haunted by the ghosts of a headless man and headless dog. The hill is regarded by some of the locals as a sinister place, where birds never sing; however, when the late Clarence Daniel visited the spot he found it 'bathed in the golden splendour of spring sunshine, and feathered minstrels appeared to have congregated there for a special festival of song, as though to refute the suggestion that birds never sang on Wenley Hill.' Wenley may take its name, like the nearby village of Wensley, from the Germanic pagan god Woden. Written as 'Wodnesleie' in 1086, the name may mean 'grove dedicated to the service of Woden'.

In the village itself, Old Hall Farm is haunted by a ghost known as the 'Grey Lady', whilst Youlgreave Hall has the 'Duel Room', where a ghostly struggle is said to take place between a Roundhead and a Cavalier, who allegedly fought to their deaths one night during the English Civil War. On the anniversary of the duel, on a dark November night, they are said to reappear, two phantom forms locked in a timeless combat. Another ghost is said to haunt the road between Youlgreave and Middleton, in the area of Roughwood Hollow; here, a phantom coach and horses have been seen, sometimes illuminated by lamps and at other times accompanied by running dogs, one witness testifying that he felt a 'strong draught' as the horses and vehicle swept past him.

Arbor Low stone circle – the 'Stonehenge of the Peak'

Arbor Low stone circle, which is affectionately known as the 'Stonehenge of the Peak', lies just over two miles west of Youlgreave, on exposed Middleton Moor, 1,230 feet above sea level. From the henge, which looks like a huge clockface from the air, a great panorama of hills and moor including the Morridge, White Edge and Stanage can be seen. The name Arbor Low is thought to derive from the Old English 'eoroburh-hlaw', meaning 'the earthwork mound', and the earthwork platform upon which the stones rest is 250 feet in diameter, surrounded by a circular ditch and bank through which two entrances are cut, north and south. The great henge monument, with its central ring of over fifty huge limestone blocks, was probably the religious focus for the tribes inhabiting the Peak District in prehistory. Construction of the henge is thought to have begun between 2500 BC and 1700 BC, and there are several Bronze Age barrows in the vicinity, including an important burial mound, perhaps the final resting place of a chieftain or priest, which cuts into the eastern side of the henge bank.

Limited excavations have taken place at the site through the ages, during which a sparse assemblage of artefacts, including broken pots and a flint dagger, as well as burnt human remains, have been discovered. A complete human skeleton was excavated near the centre of the circle, and the position of the body may indicate that this was a human sacrifice. The question of whether the stones in the circle ever stood upright remains controversial, but the balance of evidence indicates that they did, as the Revd Samuel Pegge, writing in 1783, recorded the testimony of a local man, then aged fifty, who stated that some of the stones were still standing in his memory. Forty years later another writer spoke to his son, William Normanshaw, then aged seventy-four, who 'says he had repeatedly heard his father (who died about twenty years ago at the age of ninety) say that he remembered the stones in the circle at Arborlow, many of them standing, more erect than they are now.'

Three-hundred-and-fifty yards away from the henge to the west is Gib Hill, the largest barrow in Derbyshire, so named in an eighteenth-century document 'for that a man was hung in a gibbet there first for a murder there committed'. Despite a small cist containing human remains being discovered near the top of the barrow by Thomas Bateman in the nineteenth century, the hill itself does not appear to have functioned as a burial mound. Bateman's excavation found that the 'barrow' had been constructed above four smaller mounds, which were covered with layers of burnt material including animal bones and foliage.

The function and purpose behind the Arbor Low complex remains a mystery, though as Bateman wrote in 1848:

. . . were it not for a few stone walls which intervene in the foreground, the solitude of the place and the boundless views are such as almost carry the observer back through a multitude of centuries and make him believe that he sees the same view and the same state of things as existed in the days of the architects of this once holy place.

It is not suprising in such an environment that some people sense a mystical connection with their long-dead pagan ancestors who once worshipped at this temple of the sun. To this day many people believe that Arbor Low and the other stone circles in Derbyshire are focuses of 'earth energy', the cross-over points in the alleged system of 'ley lines', ancient landscape alignments which utilise many different kinds of marker points of varying ages, constructed by ancient man in a past 'Golden Age'. Typical of the psychic experiences reported by visitors to Arbor Low is that of 'a very sincere man' who told journalist Paul Screeton how he had spent a night at the circle, and had been awakened by the ghosts of those who had constructed it who explained to him 'its purpose and dimensions'.

Many guidebooks have made the statement that 'between 50 and 150 leys' originate or feature Arbor Low as an alignment point, but Paul Devereux and Ian Thompson, in *The Ley Hunter's Companion,* were able to find only two which satisfied them. On a more scientific level, members of a research team known as the Dragon Project have used sophisticated electronic monitoring apparatus at prehistoric sites throughout the country since the late 1970s, and have detected many kinds of anomalous energy, including ultrasound and radiation emitted by standing stones at certain times of the year. Indeed, when the archaeologist Dr John Barnatt was surveying Arbor Low during the research for his book *Stone Circles of the Peak*, he was told by a man visiting the site that skylarks were attracted to the henge and others on the moors due to the ultrasound which such places emitted!

Dr Barnatt concluded that the henge was constructed with a precise geometry, so that its two entrances were aligned with the sun and moon at the summer and winter solstices, with the axes marking the rising and setting points of the sun on both occasions. The circle was also aligned in combination with other prehistoric sites, as close by ran an important prehistoric trackway which connected it with the Neolithic burial chamber at Minninglow to the south, and with the Bull Ring (another henge similar to Arbor Low, now lacking its stones) at Doveholes, north of Buxton.

Whatever mystical power or energy may lie hidden today in the landscape of Arbor Low, as one writer has observed: '. . . it is difficult not to feel something of the power and mystery of the place, for this windy ridge was clearly a focal point for prehistoric men with a crucial place in their ceremonial lives, for almost a thousand years.'

Locally, Arbor Low was once avoided after dark, as it was said to be haunted by spirits of the dead. In *Romances of the Peak*, W. M. Turner describes how:

. . . coming away from a visit there in the year 1897, I accosted a young herdsman, who was attending some cattle grazing by the wayside. After touching on several points I came cautiously to the Druidical circle business. I wanted to know how it came there and its purpose and so forth. He could not tell. It had been there undisturbed for generations and according to the account given him by the old people, and that was all, excepting, there may have been a battle there and people had been buried about the place.

'How did he come to know that?' 'Well, you see', he said, 'the folks round about never go that way at night for fear of boggarts. Several have been seen prowling about, and it is the common talk that people must have been buried there'. 'Did you ever go that way at night?' I asked. He said that he had not, but he bravely added, he would not mind, for he did not believe in such things.

Arbor Low was not the only mystical or religious focus for the inhabitants of the White Peak during the prehistoric past. On Harthill Moor, between Youlgreave and Winster, is a field known as Nine Stones Close, so named because of the ancient stone circle which survives there in a sloping meadow, overlooked by a rock escarpment known as Robin Hood's Stride. Glover, writing in 1829, stated that:

> . . . in a field north of Graned Tor, called Nine Stone Close, are the remains of a Druidical circle, about thirteen yards in diameter, now consisting of seven rude stones of various dimensions; one of them is about eight feet in height and nine in circumference. Between 70 and 80 yards to the south are two other stones, of similar dimensions, standing erect.

Today, there are only four stones remaining, with a fifth now acting as a gatepost in a field-wall to the south. The stones were also known as the Grey Ladies, and folklore describes how on moonlit nights, they can be seen to spin and move in a lumbering dance at midnight. Despite the five missing stones, the site has the largest prehistoric standing stones in the entire Peak District. Earlier this century, two of the stones had fallen and these were re-erected by J. P. Heathcote and members of the Derbyshire Archaeological Society in 1939.

In *Mysterious Derbyshire*, Rickman and Nown described Nine Stones Close as 'Derbyshire's most magical ancient site' and, with the southern horizon dominated by the curious gritstone formation known as Robin Hood's Stride, few would disagree with their statement. The Stride was considered by some antiquarians as having connections with the Druids, and is also known as Mock Beggar's Hall, perhaps as a result of the two rock 'chimneys' which rise from the summit of the crag, eighteen feet high and twenty-two feet apart, which have been nick-named 'Weasel' and 'Inaccessible' by climbers. Robin Hood in this case seems to relate not to the mystical medieval outlaw, but to the Green Man, a nature spirit. A local legend relates how Robin Hood, in the form of a giant, stood astride the rocks, with one foot on each of the pillars, and passed water onto the meadows below, 'where seven maidens, upon witnessing this, were all turned to stone'. A similar petrification legend is attached to the nearby Nine Ladies stone circle on Stanton Moor.

In his *Stone Circles of the Peak* Dr John Barnatt speculates that Nine Stones Close was carefully positioned by its builders in the Bronze Age so that the Stride could be utilised to study the movement of the moon, as the main alignment of the circle was the midsummer full-moon maximum, as seen from the circle between the two pillars of rock on the Stride. As further evidence that the Stride was a structure of mystical significance in the past is the presence of cup-and-ring markings, recently discovered, on its rocks. These enigmatic carvings date from the Bronze Age and are thought to be a prehistoric attempt to depict the movements of the moon and stars, essential for the early farmers.

Nine Stones Close is traditionally supposed to be the haunt of fairies. Derbyshire antiquarian Llewellyn Jewitt, writing in the late nineteenth century, described how:

> ... around this Druidical circle it is said – and believed by some of the people of the district – the fairies meet on certain occasions – the full moon, I believe, at midnight, and dance and hold 'high jubilee'. So firmly is this believed that I have been told with extreme seriousness of people who, passing at that time of night, have not only seen the dance but heard the 'fairy pipes' playing for them to dance to. I have heard it seriously affirmed that there were 'hundreds of fairies', gentlemen and ladies, some dancing, others sitting on the stones or on the grass around and others playing the music ...

Jewitt also describes how one day a farm labourer experienced a psychic, or hallucinogenic, experience of visiting 'fairyland', the ancient Otherworld of the Celts, whilst resting against one of the fallen stones of the circle. He had found a 'fairy pipe', a type of clay pipe popular among labourers in the Middle Ages and often turned up by the plough in Derbyshire fields. After cleaning it out he began to smoke tobacco from it. This appeared to be no ordinary kind of tobacco, for it had a 'peculiarly sweet and delicious scent more fragrant than any he had experienced from any other pipe'. Presently, he felt a strange sensation and when his eyes cleared, he:

> ... found he had the power of seeing what no mortal before had ever seen ... in front of him, beneath a large stone, he saw, as it were,

the ground transparent and far below, deep down beneath the surface was another world, more beautiful than anything he had ever dreamed of – rocks, and trees, and streams, and flowers, and palaces, and beautiful birds were not a tithe of what he saw; and more beautiful still, there were hundreds upon hundreds of 'small people' gaily dressed, and enjoying and disporting themselves in every imaginable way. It was perfectly fairyland. How long he sat there watching these little folks and admiring their subterranean world of beauties, he did not know; but at length the film came back gradually upon his eyes, the smarting returned, the vision passed away, and, his pipe gone out, he was once more able to see as of old.

The magical reputation of the area appears to have survived into medieval times, when a hermit took up residence in a cave behind Cratcliffe Tor, perhaps to seek a spiritual experience of his own. The Hermit's Cave can be seen today, with its crucifix carved in stone and a small niche thought to have held a lamp. A record of 1549 mentions a payment 'unto ye harmytt for ye brengynge of V Coppull of Counys frome Bradley to Haddon'. The cave is sheltered by a yew tree, symbol of everlasting life, and there are stories of a ghostly cowled monk who has been seen there. Between Cratcliffe Tor and Robin Hood's Stride runs the Portway, one of Derbyshire's oldest trackways, and nearby behind Harthill Farm is Castle Ring, a prehistoric earthwork, as well as a number of hut platforms of the Romano-British era.

Across the valley to the east is another striking pile of gritstone at the village of Birchover, called Rowtor Rocks. Birchover means 'the birch covered steep slope', accurately describing the gritstone ridge which has been given a bizarre appearance by the work of erosion and the hand of man, namely the Revd Thomas Eyre who lived at Rowtor Hall during the seventeenth century. He and friends converted the rocks into a retreat by carving crude chairs and steps into the outcrop in order to 'admire the view'. Local folklore gives a different reason, that he was in fact a dabbler in witchcraft, and if this was true then he may have been perpetuating the belief that Rowtor Rocks had previously been a place of pagan worship, due to its connection with the Druids. Sheltering beneath the rocks today is the well-known Druid Inn, a base for visitors who wish to scramble on the rocks, which are covered with natural basins and seventeenth-century carvings, as well as more ancient cup-and-ring marks of Bronze Age date, some of which resemble the 'passage grave' art-style found in chambered cairns of the Boyne Valley in Ireland. Perhaps the link

Rowtor Rocks, Birchover

with the Druids may have more truth to it than has been given credence, but whatever the case the large 'rocking stone', which could be moved with one hand, is no longer in evidence thanks to a gang of young men who toppled it in 1799.

In the shadow of Rowtor Rocks to the south is the tiny church of St Michael and All Angels, erected by Thomas Eyre as his own private chapel around the year 1700, according to local folklore, as penance for previous dabblings with witchcraft. Built into the porch wall of the church is a collection of carved stones, including examples of Celtic-style cult heads and herring-bone masonry. According to the church guide, the heads and stones 'were found by the writer in the walls around the fields' in the vicinity of an earlier church which stood at Upper-town, dating from the Norman period or earlier. The exact site of the old chapel is not known today, but it is thought to have been in an old field called Allen's Croft; a reference in a charter dated 1300 states that a rent of one farthing in silver was to be paid yearly 'in the chapel of Birchover on Michaelmas Day'.

Stanton Moor – 'a lost world'
The villages of Birchover, Stanton-in-the-Peak and Stanton Lees all surround the high gritstone expanse of Stanton Moor, an exposed wilderness which has been described as 'like a lost world', sacred to ancient man during the Stone and Bronze Ages. The high moor is

46

detached from the surrounding uplands by the River Derwent which flows below it to the east, and was mentioned by Bateman in 1848 as 'a rocky and uncultivated waste, about two miles in length and one-and-a-half in breadth [containing] numerous remains of antiquity, as rocking-stones, barrows, circles of erect stones, etc., of undoubted British origin'.

The moor probably functioned as a burial ground and centre of religious life and astronomical observation during the Bronze Age, between 2000 and 1500 BC, from which most of the finds are dated. Scattered amongst the heather and birch are the remains of over five stone circles (only one of which has standing stones of note), and over seventy Bronze Age barrows. Many of these have been excavated by two local archaeologists, the Heathcotes, a father and son team, earlier this century, and some of their finds can be seen in the village museum at Birchover. Among the finds were cremated remains in collared urns, battle-axes and exotic faience beads which were once thought to have originated in the eastern Mediterranean. These were uncovered at the small Doll Tor stone circle on the edge of the moor, set in a landscape alignment with Nine Stones Close across the valley on Harthill Moor.

In 1939, during the excavation of the circle by the Heathcotes, a weird incident occurred, as 'before the excavations were completely finished three of the stones were maliciously damaged by some unknown person'! The large stones involved were discovered smashed to fragments after the site had been left overnight, and had to be delicately cemented together by the excavators the following day. No explanation could be found, and the incident remains a mystery; however, folklore often warns how those who interfere with standing stones and barrows will bring about violent retribution from paranormal agencies.

There is little doubt that the pagan sanctity of the moor played an important part in local folklore during the Middle Ages. The parish records of Youlgreave Church refer to an occasion in the year 1779 when money was paid 'To Ale and bread and chees to ye men that went with the Corpes . . . For ceredge of the Corpes on to Stanton More'. This is thought to refer to the burial of a suicide or a witch, for it was the custom for such people to be buried at a cross road or at a remote or pre-Christian part of the parish, away from consecrated ground. Bodies of suicides were traditionally buried at cross roads in the hope that this would lay the ghost and prevent it from returning to the village.

Nine Ladies stone circle – in folklore, dancers turned to stone

Without a doubt, the most famous landmark on the moor is the Nine Ladies stone circle, the main attraction for most modern visitors, especially now the hideous stone wall which once surrounded it has been demolished. The circle consists of a complete ring of nine standing stones, thirty-five feet in diameter, set on the inner edge of a low bank around a shallow mound. A hundred and thirty feet away from the circle to the south-west is the 'King Stone', a lone monolith which relates to the legend from which the circle is named. Like many other stone circles in the British Isles, folklore attributes the stones to a circle of dancing maidens with the king being the fiddler, who at some time in the past were turned to stone for the crime of dancing on the Sabbath. Today the stone circle is a frequent meeting place of modern pagans as well as local witches, and dancing still takes place, especially at the break of dawn on May Day, when the Derby Morris Men perform there for the edification of early risers.

The Morris dance may preserve an earlier prehistoric fertility dance to which the legend of petrification may refer. Peter Naylor writes in *Celtic Derbyshire* that the prehistoric Peak-dwellers

'worshipped stones in various forms; monoliths, menhirs and circles
. . . there is evidence that the Celts danced around standing stones
forming a circle of people, holding hands in an unbroken chain [as] it
was believed to be a means of gaining power from a monolith.' There
were certainly a number of such sacred stones, both of a natural and
man-made nature on Stanton Moor. One such is the Cork Stone,
which stands ten feet high near a disused quarry in the centre of the
moor; although it looks as if it has been erected by man (an
impression enhanced by the metal hand-holes put there to aid
climbers), the outcrop is completely natural. It may have been a
sacred object to ancient man, for a document of 1789 states that the
Cork Stone was surrounded by four other standing stones; not far
away are more stones and a large block known as the Andle Stone, all
visible from Derwent Valley below.

Only a mile away from Stanton Moor in the valley is an ancient
church dedicated to St Helen at Churchtown in Darley Dale, one of
the most interesting in the Peak District, as an example of the
evolution of a pagan cult centre into a Christian church. The church is

St Helen's Church, Darley Dale

said to have been founded early in the tenth century during the reign of Edward the Elder, and although no trace of the Saxon church remains, the present part-Norman cruciform structure is built upon an artificial mound by the banks of the River Derwent. There are many connections to the pagan past in the church, including carved heads and a Sheela-na-gig fertility carving on the tower arch and, inside the tower, a grotesque carving of a grinning bearded face.

There is little doubt that the site of the church was of considerable importance at an early date, for before Christianity reached the area it would seem that the site of the present church was imbued with some mystical significance; there appear to have been burials of Roman date on the site, and according to one writer 'at least one human sacrifice'. As a testament to its importance in the past, in the Domesday survey of 1086 Darley is described as having a church and a priest, and shortly afterwards it had three priests.

In the churchyard stands one of the most famous yew trees in the country – estimates of its age vary from 600 to 2,000 years, but most probably it dates from Romano-British or Saxon times, when the tree could have been a cult centre perhaps connected with a river sanctuary. Whatever its precise age, according to the plaque which accompanies it today:

> . . . there can be little doubt that this grand old tree has given shelter to the early Britons when planning the construction of the dwellings which they erected not many yards to the west of its trunk. To the Romans who built up the funeral pyres for their slain companions just clear of its branches. To the Saxons, converted perchance to the true faith by the preaching of Bishop Diuma beneath its pleasant shade. To the Norman masons carving their quaint sculptures to form the first stone house of prayer, and to the host of Christian worshippers, who from that day to this, have been borne under its hoary limbs in women's arms, to the baptismal font and then on men's shoulders to their last sleeping place in the soil that gave it birth.

Outside, an ancient road skirts the spooky churchyard – this is Ghost Lane, named from the ghost of a pedlar murdered in the seventeenth century only 150 yards from the gates of the church. His ghost is said to appear periodically, haunting the bend in the lane near a large sycamore tree. Another ghost story concerns the Moor Farm Sporting Club, in Flash Lane on Matlock Moor above Darley Dale. Many centuries ago this was the site of a lonely wayside inn

The ancient Darley Yew, symbol of everlasting life

called The Quiet Woman, and for years this place had the reputation of being haunted by a headless woman, supposedly the ghost of a landlady of the Elizabethan age who had the habit of murdering unsuspecting travellers who stopped there overnight. Eventually, her gruesome secret was discovered and she was hanged and beheaded. Another version of the story runs that the ghost was the daughter of the landlord, responsible for the death of her father in a fire at the inn. Either way, both versions of the story agree that afterwards the building was repeatedly destroyed by fire, with the premises being rebuilt on the ruins and then raised to the ground again by strange conflagrations as late as 1966, after the pub had been converted into a country club.

The present chapel dedicated to St Margaret in the hamlet of Alderwasley on the hillside above Crich dates to the sixteenth century, when it functioned as the private chapel of the Hurt family. The chapel is said to be haunted, and people living nearby have heard the sound of singing emanating from the empty and disused building, as well as shuffling footsteps and a doorbell ringing although no one is there. Clarence Daniel notes that 'such a village ought to be haunted, for it has a field called Killcroft and the farm with the name of Buryhill Farm – place-names which must have been born out of some sinister circumstances in the past.'

The chapel, which stands on an earlier sacred site, is rich in carved stones which came from an older building on the same site; the south wall is adorned with carved stone heads which grimace and stare wild-eyed. On one corner is a 'Sheela-na-gig', an example of medieval pornography, believed by some authorities to be representations of the Celtic goddess of creation and destruction. Carvings such as these are common in Irish castles and churches, and their blatant sexual nature quite obviously has little to do with the Christian religion, despite the fact that they are found widely in churches. In Derbyshire there are examples in Melbourne Church, Darley Church and the stables of Haddon Hall. Sheela-na-gigs seem to perform the same function as gargoyles, and were given horrific forms to frighten away evil spirits. Some early churches may have acted as centres where pagan images were brought from the surrounding countryside to be Christianised. The Norman church at Brassington, near Wirksworth, is a good example. There are many fine carved heads and hidden from sight inside the clocktower is a carving of a strange horned figure – described by the guide as 'the oldest stone in the church'. Is this an image of the pagan god whose shrine the church replaced?

The Quiet Woman public house, Earl Sterndale

Headless phantoms of Peakland

Stories about 'headless ghosts' – some with heads in their hands, or tucked under the arms – are very common in English folklore, and some scholars believe that these legends may derive from the ancient custom of decapitating the dead, especially in the case of criminals, suicides and witches, in the belief that a headless ghost could do no harm. In the Peak District there are many headless ghost stories enshrined in local folklore – some of them having a humorous twist. South-west of Buxton, in the village of Earl Sterndale, is a public house called The Quiet Woman, whose signboard depicts a lady in a long Elizabethan costume minus her head! One version of the legend attached to the name explains how the landlord, tired of the constant chattering of his wife, cut off her head; the motto underneath the sign reading 'Soft Words Turneth Away Wrath'.

In eastern Derbyshire, between Chesterfield and Matlock, is the village of Ashover. Like several other villages in the area, the church at Ashover (which is mentioned in the Domesday Book) is said to be haunted by a 'headless woman', and it is said that not so many years ago, nothing could induce the residents of the village to walk through

Ashover Church – haunted by a 'headless woman'

the churchyard after dark. The spectre was last reported in the year 1890, when the headless lady was seen in the north aisle of the church at eight o'clock one evening. The emphasis upon the headless nature of this phantom is interesting, as it is recorded that in 1879, during the building of a conservatory at Stubben Edge Hall, to the south of the village, a human skull was discovered by the workmen, arousing much speculation about its origins. One theory was that the skull came originally from Ashover churchyard, from which it had been brought twenty years before as part of a wager. Could it be that the ghost of its owner, deprived of her head, haunts the church as a consequence? Whatever the explanation, there is a local record that in 1841 a farmer, John Towndrow, 'murdered his wife with a hammer and cut her head off; he afterwards cut his throat. He was buried at 9 o'clock at night, after the verdict of the Jury, and put into his coffin with all his clothes on except his shoes'.

A similar story is told of the ghost of Stoke Hall, once the Peakland residence of the Earls of Bradford. Constructed in 1755, on the banks of the River Derwent near the village of Grindleford, the hall has always had the reputation of being haunted by a multitude of

Stoke Hall, Grindleford

spectres. A headless ghost has been reported by several visitors to the hall, which has now been converted into a country hotel; one lady visiting the hall in the 1880s to attend a feast saw, as she made her way to bed late at night, 'a lady in a beautiful dress coming down the staircase'. The spectral figure had no head and disappeared as the lady screamed and fell to the floor. R. Murray Gilchrist, describing the hall, mentions how 'the neighbouring folk in former years used to tell a weird story of a skull that haunted the upper storey, and one may be sure that they feared to pass alone after edge o'the dark.'

The ghost of the hall is believed locally, according to Gilchrist, to be that of 'Fair Flora', a young lady who was murdered in, or near, the hall many years ago either by a jealous lover or by a band of gypsies. The owners of the hall are said to have been so shocked by the death of the girl that they erected a statue of her in the garden to commemorate her. The statue, which is in fact a carving of Flora, the Greek goddess of flowers, came originally from Chatsworth House as a gift to a Mrs Taylor, a former owner of the hall. The erection of the statue in the garden, however, led to a spate of bad luck and it is said that in the twilight the statue took on a ghostly appearance, and on occasions was seen to move. For this reason Fair Flora was removed some years ago to the north of the hall, where it now stands, headless, on a lonely hillside overlooking the village of Grindleford. Perhaps as a result of local superstition, Fair Flora has been decapitated and despite its replacement, according to Clarence Daniel, 'on each occasion the head was again forcibly dislodged, so now [the statue] is in the custody of a sympathetic resident who protects it from further damage.'

Former workers at the hall tell many different versions of this story. One version describes how an heiress to the property was murdered in the hall; her ghost haunts a particular room where indelible bloodstains remain; strange rustling noises are often heard, and even today there are reports of strange phenomena including the mysterious ringing of bells and the triggering of a burglar alarm without any explanation being found. A few hundred yards from the hall, near the banks of the river, are the ruins of a cottage which are haunted by the ghost of a carrier, Old Ned, who is said to have hanged himself there. His ghost is seen at midnight 'tearing off branches from the trees, and finally disappearing over the crumbling walls into the ruins'.

More headless ghosts are credited with haunting the quaint village of Winster, famous for its medieval brick and stone Market House, once the centre of the local lead-mining industry. Opposite is a privately-owned building which was once an old coaching inn known as The Angel. The three-storey building is said to be haunted by the ghost of a headless bride, who was seen by a lady many years ago descending the upper flight of stairs to the landing outside her bedroom door. More recently other unexplained happenings have been reported from the house, including strange footsteps and doors opening and closing by themselves.

Only a few hundred yards away down the street is Winster Hall, now a public house but once the home of Llewellyn Jewitt, a famous antiquarian and collector of Derbyshire folklore. The hall is haunted by the ghosts of a woman and her lover, a coachman whom she had been forbidden to marry. The story tells how they flung themselves to their deaths from the top of the hall and were afterwards buried in the grounds. The ghost of the lady victim of the suicide pact has been sighted in the forecourt of the hall, and, according to Clarence Daniel, when soldiers were billeted in the building during the last war, 'one of them was so convinced that he had seen a ghost that he fired a revolver and the bullet was found embedded in the wooden shutters of the window'.

Buxton and the South-western Moors

Buxton, Chapel-en-le-Frith and the western moorlands

Harpur Hill, near Buxton, was once the haunt of a boggart known as 'the ghost of Ben Stiles'. A wild, heathy piece of land stretches out from the quarry near the village to a place known as 'The Frith', where an old stile was the scene of a murder many years ago. According to William Turner, writing 1901, 'the poor victim was named Ben and, in the absence of a surname, he has been dubbed Stiles by the country-people, owing to the fact that his body was found at or near this particular stile'. The ghost was said to appear 'at any time after sunset and before the dawn of day', though can only be seen by 'privileged persons', or those with psychic powers. A ghostly nun haunted Yhelt Cottage, near Buxton, dating to the sixteenth century and supposedly built near the site of an old nunnery. Strange rosy lights have been seen here inside one of the bedrooms, and in 1953 'the ghost of a nun surrounded by a bright, unearthly illumination' was seen by the owners: 'She looked about twenty-eight years old and was extremely beautiful'.

The spa town of Buxton itself may once have been the site of a shrine to a powerful pagan water goddess known as Arnemetia. The Romans named their settlement at Buxton 'Aquae Arnemetiae'. Peter Naylor, in *Ancient Wells and Springs of Derbyshire*, notes that Buxton was one of only two places in Roman Britain with the name 'Aquae', the other being the famous temple of Sulis-Minerva at Bath. The two major springs at Buxton, one hot and one cold, have been venerated as a centre for healing and pilgrimage for thousands of years. Although many guidebooks credit the Romans with the discovery of the waters, archaeology and the place-name itself indicate that the shrine originated in the Iron Age, as a temple in a sacred grove dedicated to the Celtic water goddess, Arnemetia, from which the present holy well takes its name, Christianised as St Ann.

St Ann's Well, Buxton – 'Aquae Arnemetiae' to the Romans

Roman brickwork and a stone carving of the goddess were discovered in the well during exacavations in the seventeenth century, and more recently Roman coins have been uncovered, indicating that the waters have been used from time immemorial for their healing properties. At the height of the town's fame as a spa, the thermal waters at Buxton were visited by 10–12,000 people per year, one of whom, in the sixteenth century, was the ill-fated Mary Queen of Scots, then in the custody of the Earl of Shrewsbury at Sheffield.

St Ann's Well was at one time believed to be the source of the River Wye, but in fact the true source is within the subterranean chambers beneath Poole's Cavern on the moors, to the south-west of the town. This natural cavern, famous for its spectacular stalactites, the largest of which is known as the 'Flitch of Bacon', takes its name from an outlaw known as Poole, who is supposed to have lived in the cave around the year 1440, during the reign of King Henry VI. Legend has it that Poole used the cave as a base for his operations, storing his loot there and hiding from pursuers.

Many hundreds of years before, during the Iron Age, Poole's Cavern was used as a shelter and hideaway for the local Celtic tribes.

Poole's Cavern, Buxton – one of the 'Seven Wonders of the Peak'

It was probably also used as a burial ground – as the large Grin Low prehistoric barrow on the hill above the cavern suggests. Excavations inside the cavern in the nineteenth century, and more recently during the 1980s, have uncovered evidence that the Romans as well as the native tribes regarded the cavern entrance as sacred. Bones, skulls, pottery and some Roman jewellery and coins were found in the entrance chamber during the early digs, and since 1981 archaeologists have uncovered over one hundred examples of bronze brooches in the form of dolphins and sea-horses, discs resembling chariot-wheels, as well as small collections of pins. It is now thought likely that the 'Roman Chamber' was the site of a shrine where both Romans and Celts alike came to worship subterranean water-gods. So many items in bronze have been discovered that there is even a suggestion that a workshop once existed in the cave entrance, producing jewellery and metalwork. This is not unusual in the area, for rope-makers once lived in small cottages in the mouth of Peak Cavern at Castleton.

Caves and caverns throughout the Peak were in the past given a supernatural reputation – they were believed to be inhabited by the Devil, as was the case at Peak Cavern at Castleton, or by giants, as at Giant's Hole, a pothole nearby. At Peak Forest, on the limestone plateau between Buxton and Castleton, lies an awesome yawning cavern known as Eldon Hole, the largest open pothole in Derbyshire. Eldon Hole and Eldon Hill nearby, the site of a prehistoric barrow, take their name from 'elves' hill', first recorded in the thirteenth century. The immense limestone cavity, listed as one of the 'Seven Wonders of the Peak' by the poet Charles Cotton in 1682, at one time had a fearsome reputation, for it was thought to be bottomless and the habitation of evil spirits. It is said that the Earl of Leicester, in the sixteenth century, caused a man to be lowered down on a rope to ascertain its true depth, but the poor fellow went crazy and could give no account of his experience, dying shortly afterwards. We now know that the pothole is 245 feet deep, after it was first explored in 1780. The hole is also the last resting place of a traveller who was thrown over the edge after being robbed by two villains in the eighteenth century.

Barrows or lows (from the Saxon 'hlaw', meaning burial mound) dating from the Neolithic and Bronze Ages, are very common throughout the limestone uplands in the Peak District, and were connected with fairies and hobgoblins, the ghosts of those buried thousands of years ago. Often the names of barrows betray this connection, as in the mound known as Hob Hurst's House on Baslow Moor in eastern Derbyshire. On the western moorlands is Cauldon Low, the subject of a poem by Mary Howitt, *The Fairies of Cauldon Low*. This mound was believed to be inhabited at certain times of the year by the little people. The fairies of Long Low, behind Castern Hall, were said to dance and hold high revel on Christmas eve, whilst evidence of a similar belief exists at the now-levelled Goodfellow Bank in the market town of Leek.

A whole clan of fairies was said to inhabit the cavern known as Lud's Church, a dramatic gritstone rock chasm on the Staffordshire-Cheshire border near Wincle. The dramatic rocky cleft is the result of a geological fault, extending 200 feet into the hillside, whose steep stone steps extend downwards in the dark and dank cavern, fifty feet deep and nine feet wide. The cave, or 'church', for neither term seems entirely appropriate, is hidden on the western slopes of Back Forest in the Dane Valley. Here, legends abound describing the secret religious ceremonies held in Lud's Church in the fifteenth century, when it was a haven for followers of the heretical preacher Robert Wycliff. The 'church' is said to have derived its name from Walter de Ludauk, a follower of Wycliff, who held secret religious services here and was captured along with many of his followers when surprised by government troops; during the skirmish his granddaughter is said to have been killed and buried in the entrance to the cave, where for many years stood a statue of a woman known as 'Lady Lud'.

It is more likely that the name is derived from that of the Celtic sun god Lugh – 'Lugh of the Long Hand' to the Irish, whose name survived in the summer festival known as Lughnasa, on 1 August, when farmers would traditionally trade their stock, and village fairs would be held. Lud's Church was recently identified as the legendary Green Chapel, a cornerstone of the classic medieval saga *Sir Gawain and the Green Knight*. Here, the hero of the late fourteenth-century Arthurian romance slew the Green Knight, symbolic of death, rebirth and fertility. Some authorities believe that originally he may have been the old sun god or the Green Man, whose decapitation and revival represent the annual death and rebirth of vegetation.

In the Gawain saga the Green Chapel (Lud's Church) is described as 'a worn barrow on a brae by the brink of a water', which suggests the presence of a pagan burial place. A stone on the path which leads out of the cavern towards the River Dane is said to be the remains of an altar where sacrifices were made to the gods in the past. It is to be expected that the vicinity of Lud's Church would be haunted by all

Lud's Church – the 'Green Chapel' of Arthurian legend?

manner of ghosts and boggarts; thus, there are stories of headless green men and strange floating lights. Last century, tales were told of the 'Ghost of the Back Forest', which haunted the vicinity of Lud's Church and terrified night-travellers as they wound along through the trees towards Castle Cliff. There was also the 'Bosley Boggart', a terrible ghost whose fame spread terror through the countryside for miles. These are only a few examples of the stories which, according to a contributor to *The Reliquary* in the 1860s, 'are told by the lowest and most ignorant of the inhabitants, and such too, as the older and more intelligent will neither believe nor repeat'.

The activities of ghosts and spirits were once a part of everyday life in the western moorlands region of the Peak, and local folklore reflects this rich heritage – there are stories of ghostly black dogs, weird dancing lights and malicious boggarts. Most fearsome of all the spectres of this region is the phantom of a headless horseman, riding a ghostly white horse, who is reputed to gallop along the Manifold Valley on moonlit nights; one country fellow who saw the ghost at a crossroads in the 1930s described it as 'a man on a horse without a yed on, an awful gory sight!' This terrible spectre travels the road from Onecote over Butterton Moor to Warslow, and is said to be either the ghost of a pedlar murdered by robbers, who, for a joke severed his head and set the headless body on a horse, or the spirit of a knight killed in battle with the Scots, whose horse brought the headless body of his master home. 'Phantom coaches' have also been reported in the region; the 'Cromwell Coach' rides along the lane from Ilam to Throwley, above the Manifold ravine in Dovedale. In daytime it is heard but not seen, whilst at night 'one can see its lights'. Another coach haunted the road between Ashbourne and Leek at Low Hill, once again being heard but not seen.

The road between Leek and Buxton crosses the bleak Morridge moors, where locals tell stories of the Mermaid of Blake Mere or Black Meer, a story told elsewhere in the High Peak, concerning Mermaid's Pool on Kinder Scout. The Blake Mere mermaid, so it is said, appears at midnight to drag unsuspecting visitors beneath the acidic waters which are said to be bottomless. Nearby is an old drover's inn, the Mermaid Inn, where to this day a legend is inscribed which reads:

She calls on you to greet her
combing her dripping crown,
and if you go to greet her,
She ups and drags you down . . .

The mere has certainly been the setting for two recorded murders or attempted murders, and legends such as these appear to be relics of a time when gods and nature spirits were an important part of the cycle of life and death to Peaklanders. Some scholars believe that the eerie stories told about sacred pools and rivers may preserve memories of human sacrifice to water gods in the distant past.

Not very far from the Morridge mere is another moorland pool where a mermaid, or water spirit is said to bathe. This is Doxey Pool on the moor above the rock escarpment known as the Roaches, which rises many hundreds of feet above any other known spring in the district. In 1949, Mrs Florence Pettit visited this pool one morning for a swim before lunch, in the company of a friend from Buxton. She wrote afterwards that just before she was to enter the water:

> . . . a great 'thing' rose up from the middle of the lake. It rose very quickly until it was 25 to 30 feet tall. Seeming to be part of the slimy weeds and the water, yet it had eyes, and those eyes were extremely malevolent. It pointed its long boney fingers menacingly at me so there was no mistaking its hostility. I stood staring at the undine, water spirit, naiad or whatever it was while my heart raced. Its feet just touched the surface of the water, the weeds and the air. When I dared to look again the creature was dissolving back into the elements from which it had formed.

Many years afterwards, when discussing her bone-chilling encounter with a local rambler, she asked him if he had ever visited the Roaches, and he replied, 'Not likely, there's a haunted lake on top'.

At the windswept village of Flash, which at 1,518 feet lays claim to be the highest in England, a house is said to have been dismantled at one time because of a persistent haunting. Nearby, at the old village of Rushton, is the 'Murder Stone', in the north-east corner of the churchyard. Here, it is said, lies the body of a youth, murdered by a doctor. The boy's ghost thereafter became so troublesome that his body had to be dug up and turned around in the grave 'with his feet to the west, in order to stop him from reappearing'. The village itself, according to one writer, derives its original name from 'the hill of the spirit'; and significantly, the old church is thought to occupy the site of a pagan temple – 'a sacred grove in heathen times, and a small spring supplied the baptismal water when its people became Christian, and changed their worship, clinging however to the same spot'. Another place-name nearby, part of Rushton, is Wormhill – 'the hill of the serpents'.

In Rushton, a tale was told last century of how a servant girl was murdered by her mistress; despite her obvious guilt the mistress escaped trial through a legal technicality. However, although she had escaped the hand of justice, the local people declared that she never had any peace thereafter, for every night the ghost of the murdered girl haunted her bedside, and would never allow her to sleep before cock-crow in the morning. At last, the tormented woman became so desperate that she gathered twelve clergymen to 'lay' the ghost by bell and by book:

> ... not withstanding the fainting of one or two, some one or other of them read away till it was quietly laid on the Cloud*-hillside, and afterwards it appeared only as a 'phantom', a dim blue light often pointed out by the coachman to night travellers.
> *[Celtic word peculiar to northern Staffordshire meaning 'hill' or 'mountain']

Will o'the Wisp, UFOs and the Phantom Helicopter
Unexplained lights known to countryfolk as the 'Will o'the Wisp' or the 'Jack o'Lantern' were common phenomena in moorland and marshy regions before the arrival of street-lighting. There have been many attempts to explain these strange moving lights as methane gas produced by rotting vegetation, which is thought to ignite spontaneously under certain conditions. This theory is unlikely to explain sightings in mountainous areas, and the rapid movement and longevity of the lights reported by those who have seen Will o'the Wisp defy the laws of physics which govern the ignition of marsh gas.

Writing in 1901, Turner in *Romances of the Peak* links Will o'the Wisp with the boggart – a mischievous ghost or fairy:

> ... between Derbyshire and Staffordshire, in the upper part of the vale of the Dove, there is a piece of marshy land called, locally, 'The Mossco-Carrs'. It is rather an eerie place to pass by in the twilight or before the dawn [as] there is a flickering light to be seen moving as one moves; and it has given rise to many tales of belated travellers having been beguiled by it and led into the swamp, where their bodies remain, and from whence their 'boggarts' arise at night to caper and dance all over the countryside, to the terror of the believing inhabitants.

Researcher Phil Reeder has described how many years ago, whilst travelling on a bus near Ashbourne in southern Derbyshire, he overheard two elderly women discussing how the countryside around had changed over the years. One said to the other that as a girl she could remember a certain field where Will o'the Wisps used to 'play'; her friend too recalled seeing them there, but added that the lights were no longer to be seen. 'At the time, the most remarkable thing to me about their conversation', writes Phil, 'was the casual way these country women had accepted the existence and regular occurrence, albeit in their youth, of a phenomenon I had thought extremely rare, if indeed it existed outside fairy tale'.

The apparent disappearance today of the Will o'the Wisps and fairies of old from the hills of the Peak and elsewhere may be a consequence of the changes which have taken place in the countryside, both to the environment and to the people themselves. For today, no doubt, if lights of this nature are seen, the observer will either keep the fact to himself or report what he has seen as a UFO – an Unidentified Flying Object. Phil Reeder notes the curious fact that while sightings of Will o'the Wisp have decreased towards the end of last century, sightings of UFOs have increased!

What can be claimed as the very first recorded sighting of an Unidentified Flying Object in the Peak District took place in the year 1716, and is recorded in the parish registers of Chapel-en-le-Frith. In an entry dated 30 March of that year it is recorded that 'between the hours of nine and twelve at night there appeared in the North and North West, a strange sort of light in the air', so bright that:

> . . . several could have read a book at that time of night . . . it streamed up like unto long picks, of a large bigness, some black, some the colour of the rainbow, some a whitish colour, and at last it broke into flashes like lightning or smoke, as if it had been smoke of guns, as fast as you could clap your hands, very terrible to behold.

This curious 'light' may have been an unusually brilliant appearance of the 'Northern Lights', the Aurora Borealis. The same night on which this appearance was noted at Chapel-en-le-Frith, it also caused considerable terror to the residents of the other Peakland villages. A similar light was seen at Hartington on 6 March that year, which caused so much alarm that it became the subject of a popular ballad, entitled 'On the Strange and Wonderful Sight that was seen in the Air on the 6th March, 1716':

The Sixth of March, kind neighbours this is true,
A Wonder in the Sky came to my view;
I pray believe it, for I tell no Lye,
There's many more did see it as well as I.

I was on Travel, and was very late,
To speak the truth just about Daylight gate;
My heart did tremble being all alone,
To see such Wonders – the like was never known.

These Lights to me like great long spears did show,
Sharp at one end, kind neighbours this is true;
I was so troubled I could not count them o'er,
But I suppose there was above a score.

Then I saw like Blood it did appear,
And that was very throng among the spears;
I thought the Sky would have opened in my View,
I was so daunted I didn't know what to do.

The next I saw two clouds meet fierce together
As if they would have fought one another;
And darkened all these spears excepting one,
They gave a clash and quickly they were gone.

The very last Day in the same month I'm told
Many People did strange Sights behold;
At Hartington, the truth I will not spare,
That night they saw Great Wonders in the Air.

This Hartington it is in Darbyshire,
And credible persons living there,
They have declared that wonders they did view
The very last night in March its certain true.

Strange aerial happenings also figure in the history of the Goyt Valley region, west of the town of Whaley Bridge. In his history of Cheshire, T. A. Coward tells of an occurrence in the late seventeenth century when 'a great pillar of smoke', said to be as high as a steeple and twenty feet broad, swept across the moorlands at Whaley, Taxal and Macclesfield Forest, making 'an hideous noise'. This terrible vortex of wind is said to have picked up stone walls and trees from a wood and carried them away, clearing haycocks, laying growing corn flat, and destroying houses before going 'up the hills into Derbyshire, and so vanished'.

In more recent years, sightings of UFOs have taken place regularly in the region. In August 1962 the *Buxton Advertiser* recorded the sighting of Michael Valance, a teacher from Chesterfield, who saw a weird object in the sky whilst driving between Glossop and Chapel-en-le-Frith; the UFO was box-shaped, with four lighted windows and surrounded by a glowing light. The object hovered over a remote moor for several minutes before disappearing in a haze.

More recently, on the evening of 31 August 1980, unexplained lights in the sky were reported by over thirty people in thirteen separate locations in the area, ranging from Hatton in southern Derbyshire to Buxton in the north and Beresford Dale, where the object was spotted by a group of campers. One of the witnesses first thought that it was an aircraft on fire, for it was surrounded by a haze or vapour. As he watched closely, he saw a hovercraft-shaped object, about the size of a jumbo jet, with portholes and shimmering bright green, white, red and blue lights. Despite a thorough investigation at the time by a UFO society based in Nottingham, no satisfactory explanation was ever found to account for these sightings.

One of the most puzzling unsolved mysteries of recent years concerns an unusual ghost which haunted the High Peak region around the town of Buxton in the winter of 1973–74. This ghost was unique, as it was dubbed by the press at the time as a 'phantom helicopter', which must rank as quite a novelty in the records of unexplained happenings!

The mystery began in September, 1973, at Harpur Hill, on the moors to the south-east of Buxton in the High Peak of Derbyshire. At one o'clock in the morning, a resident who lived opposite the large Hillhead limestone quarry observed what she perceived to be a helicopter, apparently rising directly out of the quarry, and reported the matter to the police. A security guard, Simon Crowe, also saw the phantom helicopter, and he said:

> The two best sightings I had were both in Hillhead Quarry, one about ten o'clock and the other about midnight. At no time did I positively identify it as an helicopter – apart from its ability to hover and the sound from the rotor-blades. On the first sighting it hovered at about fifty feet from the ground with spotlights shining downwards into the main quarry floor. When I approached in the landrover with my headlights on, it rose slowly and flew away

towards Mines Research. On the second occasion it rose out of the quarry and I was not aware of it until I saw the lights. It quickly disappeared in the same direction as before . . .

The headlines of the *Derbyshire Times* on 18 January 1974 read: 'Police puzzled by helicopter's mystery flights', describing how after midnight on the morning of Monday, 14 January 1974, police in the Macclesfield area of Cheshire received a report describing an unidentified 'copter, and were said to have 'kept the machine under observation for some time' as it manoeuvred over the moors towards the High Peak. Derbyshire police were alerted and at 1.00 am the crew of a patrol car spotted the 'copter flying above Mam Tor in the vale of Edale. The patrol car gave chase, but the helicopter appeared to veer off towards Sheffield, and the police soon lost it. Later the craft was said to have landed at the Cheshire village of Goostrey, near the Jodrell Bank radio-telescope.

By the middle of January 1974 up to seven separate police forces were actively involved in the investigation of the helicopter mystery. Many other sightings of the strange night-flying helicopter were made that winter, but despite extensive police investigations the pilot was never traced and the mystery remains unsolved to this day.

The phantom helicopter mystery demonstrates that experiences with the unknown are not confined to days gone by, when stories were told around the fireside to titillate the superstitious, but live on today in a slightly different form, in the articles about poltergeists and flying saucers which appear in the columns of our daily newspapers.

The Curse of Dickey's Skull
In his book *Household Tales and other Traditional Remains,* published in 1895, S. O. Addy, a collector of Derbyshire folklore, tells of an old farmhouse situated in the Royal Forest of the Peak where, it was said, two sisters once lived who loved the same man. Their rivalry ended when one sister murdered the other, but the dying sister commanded her bones would never rest in any grave:

> . . . and so it happens that her bones are kept in a 'cheese-vat' in the farmhouse which stands in a staircase window. If the bones are removed from the vat trouble comes upon the house, strange noises are heard at night, the cattle die or are seized with illness.

Although the story does not specify the name of the farmhouse, it would appear that this folk tale is the oldest-known version of the famous legend of 'Dickey O'Tunstead'. Dickey was both a human skull and a fearsome ghost, whose legendary antics were kept alive for many centuries at Tunstead Farm (part of a hamlet dating from the thirteenth century), on the hillside between the towns of Chapel-en-le-Frith and Whaley Bridge. According to Clarence Daniel, 'enough stories are told about this "Piltdown Man of the Peak" to fill a book'. Tunstead was once known locally as Skull Farm, such was the extent of fame surrounding the strange relic which, until recently, was preserved on the kitchen window-sill of the farmhouse.

'According to the evidence of many local inhabitants, the house is peaceful and quiet while the skull remains there, but if it be removed the noises recur, and a voice is heard in the wind as the latter, with strange moanings, comes through the keyholes of every door in the house, saying, "Fetch poor Dickey back... Fetch poor Dickey back...," and to this day the weird skull rests in the quiet corner of the window, and in the room a peculiar silence reigns.'

J. Castle Hall

When Hutchinson, the author of *A Tour through the High Peak*, visited Tunstead Farm and saw the skull in 1790, he was told by the current tenant, Adam Fox, that it had been in the house for 'near two centuries . . . during all the revolutions of owners and tenants in that time'. Mr Fox also told Hutchinson that he 'can produce fifty persons within the parish who have seen an apparition at this place'. Until recently the legends and stories surrounding the skull were known to almost everyone in the Chapel area, to the extent that at one time postcards were sold depicting the skull and detailing its long history.

Many legends and folk stories concern the strange skull and its powers. Some of them attempt to account for how the skull arrived at its uneasy resting-place on the kitchen window-sill of the farm, where it remained for generations. Recently, however, it is said to have been buried in the garden by the farm's present owners, who were tired of having a mouldering pile of bones in the kitchen, and the never-ending stream of visitors that they attracted.

The name of the skull connects it with the Dixon family, to whom the farm belonged for many generations from the eighteenth century until just after the Second World War. Sam Dixon, the last of the male line, 'would not talk about Dickey, for whom he had a great respect and a real fear'. Many wild stories were formerly told about the skull; the farm's owner in 1889 told William Braylsford Bunting that up until then the skull was in a perfect state of preservation, albeit in three parts, and that no dust would ever settle upon it!

The most popular version of the story, repeated in many local guidebooks, is that 'Dickey' was the skull of a soldier, Ned Dickson, who was murdered and buried on the farm by his cousins after returning from a foreign war to reclaim his inheritance. After the foul deed, every kind of misfortune fell upon the usurping couple – strange noises, crop failure and ghostly visitations. Eventually, according to one story, following the advice of a witch, Dickson's skull was dug up and given a place of honour in the homestead 'to placate the powers that be'. The involvement of a local witch is interesting, as a third and little-known tradition asserts that the skull is really that of a witch! The legend of Ned Dickson's murder at Tunstead Farm was immortalised by Derbyshire poet William Bennett early this century, in a ballad which runs:

'What's that i'the nook, John?' she suddenly cried,
And shaking with terror they clearly espied
The head of Ned Dickson upright on the stone,
As wan and as ghastly as when he was done.

Many years passed away and the murderers fell,
By just retribution as ancient folk tell;

By a blow from her husband the woman was killed,
By the fall of an oak was Jack Johnson's blood spilled.

But the head of Ned Dickson still stood in the nook,
Though they tried to remove it by bell and by book;
Though wasted of skin and flesh, still the skull
Will remain at its post till its weird be full.

Local legend warns that should the skull be taken from the farm, disaster will follow disaster until it is brought back again. Hutchinson wrote that 'twice within the memory of man the skull has been taken from the premises – once on building the present house on the site of the old one, and another time when it was buried in Chapel churchyard – but there was no peace! no rest! it had to be replaced'.

Over the two centuries since this was written, Dickey's skull has been ejected by several farmers who have occupied the house, on one occasion being thrown out onto a manure heap, but these efforts to rid the farm of its 'curse' have always been followed by strange happenings and bad luck; as late as 1980 a local author wrote that 'I have heard of many accidents happening, and without mentioning names, it has always been when the skull was moved'. On one occasion, the skull was stolen and taken to Disley, near Manchester, where it manifested its annoyance by creating so great an uproar with fearful noises that the thieves were very glad to return it to Tunstead Farm!

The only solution which would cure such outbreaks of paranormal fury was the restoration of the skull to its place of honour on the kitchen window-sill of the farm. On one occasion the skull was hurled into Coombes Reservoir but the fish are said to have died; on another it was thrown into the river but was hastily pulled out again! Holy ground was no better; the skull has twice been buried in the churchyard at Chapel-en-le-Frith, but had to be dug up again when a great storm arose and deafening noises plagued the farm – cattle died, crops failed to ripen, strange diseases spread among the flocks, and nothing prospered.

One local resident has described how:

> . . . my late grandfather, who died in 1945 aged ninety-three, often spoke of the legend of the skull which was also known as the 'weeping skull'. Legend has it that the skull was uncovered during renovations to the ancient farmhouse prior to the Reformation. It was encased in the thick rubble wall directly beneath a window

ledge. The skull was placed on the window-sill and, if it remained there, all was apparently quite peaceful. If, however, it was moved from this location there was apparently considerable noise and disturbance in and around the house including moving furniture and ornaments. At these times the skull was also said to weep and moan loudly. My grandfather, who was a very tough level-headed hill-farmer, not given to wild imaginings, claimed to have witnessed such occurrences. According to the old gentleman one resident of the house actually threw the skull out onto the midden at which all hell is supposed to have broken out. The skull is said to have screamed out whilst pandemonium reigned all around through one night. The skull is said to have rolled itself back to the house door where it tapped to be let in!

The reputation of Dickey O'Tunstead as a supernatural guardian of the farm and its lands, and as a symbol of opposition to unwelcome changes, was demonstrated powerfully in 1862, when the Northwestern Railway Company announced a plan to build a railway bridge across some land belonging to Tunstead Farm, linking Buxton with Whaley Bridge. It didn't take long for Dickey's curse to be blamed for the successive collapse of foundations built upon the unstable marshy land by the railway engineers, who were repeatedly thwarted in their attempts to build a bridge – one section is said to have collapsed overnight, burying the workmen's tools! Eventually, the railway, as well as a new road to Chapel, had to be built higher up the line at Dane Hey; here the legend has been enshrined in a local place-name: Dickey's Bridge. It was the belief that a ghost had caused a change in the route of the railway line which inspired Samuel Laycock, a Lancashire poet, to pen his 'Address to Dickie', first published in the *Buxton Advertiser* in 1870, and reprinted in Llewellyn Jewitt's *Derbyshire Ballads*:

Neaw, Dickie, be quiet wi' thee, lad,
An' let navvies an' railways a'be;
Mon tha shouldn't do soa, its too bad,
What harm are they doin' to thee?
Deed folk shouldn't meddle at o'
But leov o' these matters to th' wick;
They'll see they're done gradely, aw know-
Dos't' yer what aw say to thee, Dick?

Despite the anti-social habits of 'Dickey', the skull – like the stories describing magical heads found in Celtic mythology – responded generously to kind and respective treatment, and acted as a family talisman against bad luck and misfortune. If Dickey was treated kindly, he would harness horses, draw attention to lost sheep, warn of marauding burglars and strangers, impending illness and cows in calf. Hutchinson recorded in the nineteenth century that the 'apparition' of Dickey 'is looked upon more as a guardian spirit than a terror to the family, never disturbing them but in case of an approaching death of a relation or neighbour, and showing its resentment only when spoken of with disrespect'. One tenant of the farm even stated that he would sooner have suffered the loss of his best cow than be parted with the skull; another told a writer that she had 'recently refused an offer of £100 for the skull, which proves in what regard it is held'.

The 'Miraculous Skull', as William Wood described Dickey in his *Tales and Traditions of the High Peak* was regarded by the farm owners as their own 'guardian spirit', hence the farmlands were known as 'Dickey's Land', and as local author M. A. Bellhouse has written 'Even now, with very old people, the "hoo doo" remains, and when my mother was young, no one would dare cross Dickey's land after dusk.'

Despite its name, pathological examination of the skull earlier this century ascertained that the skull was that of a young woman; others have suggested that it may be prehistoric in origin. This theory was first suggested by Crichton Porteous in his book on Derbyshire, published in 1950: 'How old it is', he wrote, 'no-one knows, but when it was examined some years ago by a medical man it was said to show no sign of decay and he thought it was the skull of a girl about 18 years.'

The connection of a female ghost with Dickey appears to contradict the story of the murder of Ned Dickson, and may support the belief that the skull is really that of a woman murdered – or sacrificed – at Tunstead in the distant past. A female ghost appeared on one occasion to a tenant, Mr Lomas, one night when his baby daughter was lying dangerously ill. He was sitting in the kitchen, with the baby's cradle behind him when he saw a girl slip into the room, and bend over the cradle. In the candlelight, he mistook her for one of the maids. Lomas told her she could leave the baby, as he would attend to it, and upon this she instantly vanished. Shortly afterwards, so it is said, his baby daughter died. At Cadster, a nearby hamlet, there is a haunting by a ghostly 'white lady', and people returning home at dusk have seen her floating in front of their cars 'like a white shirt'.

The most interesting suggestion was that the skull may have originated from a cairn, or burial, associated with the remains of Cadster stone circle on the hillside above Tunstead Farm. Perhaps, as one writer has suggested, the skull may be that of some long-forgotten Celtic chieftain, offended at being disturbed from his last resting place, for isolated skulls and headless skeletons have been unearthed in many barrows in this area, as noted by the famous pioneer archaeologist Thomas Bateman in 1861.

The custom of preserving a skull in the walls of a farm or house recalls the frequent appearance of carved stone heads and faces – of Celtic or later origin – found throughout the Pennine hills. The tales of misfortune, bad luck and the failure of crops if the skulls are moved from their place of residence are also found in the folklore surrounding these carved cult heads; for example a stone head connected with a well at Chisworth, near Glossop, is, according to its owner, 'supposedly, not to be moved or ill-tidings will come to pass'.

The ghost of Tunstead Farm appears locally in a number of different forms, in a manner similar to the shape-shifting gods of Celtic mythology. In his account of the Dickey legend, S. O. Addy says that the 'ghost' is regarded as a blessing upon the house and 'appears in all kinds of shapes – sometimes as a dog, and sometimes as a young lady in a silk dress. In whatever form he appears, he will point to something amiss if you follow him'. The land of Tunstead Farm is the haunt of a large, black dog well known in British folklore; this phantom hound ran next to fields belonging to Tunstead Farm, known as 'Dickey's Land', and was also seen at the hamlet of Cockyard. The dog was believed locally to be the spirit of Dickey himself.

The Phantom Dog of the Peak

Margaret Bellhouse writes 'This dog appears from nowhere at the top of the hill on the road to Combs and walks behind one, right down the hill, when coming dusk. It makes no noise, acknowledges nobody, and vanishes into nothing at the bottom of the hill'. She adds:

> I have experienced this, and know it to be true, my mother also saw it, when a girl. My husband David, who lived at Rock Villa when a boy, reports that he and his brother panicked when they saw a 'small black dog' sitting on an island in the middle of flood water,

near 'Michael's Cottage'. He and his brother both experienced the same fear, and 'ran like the clappers of Hell for nigh on half a mile'.

Well might they fear, for the sighting of such a phantom dog was regarded in some areas as a sure sign of impending death. In Chapel-en-le-Frith, a 'ghost dog' was often seen at one time sitting on the corner of Horderns Road, near a railway bridge. This phantom would always follow a specific route and sit on the corner of the road. On the opposite side of the valley in the 1890s the old people told the story of the Black Dog of Ollerenshaw; he walked on or about the Ides of March, at Brooms Head, near the old hall. According to some local story-tellers there were other black dogs in the parish – one at Smithbrook and another at Barmoor Clough, the location of a famous Ebbing and Flowing Well; this ghost must have been worth meeting for it was said he 'came out of a culvert with his head under his arm'.

The phantom black dog, or 'Padfoot' as he is called in some regions, is well known in the western moorlands of the Peak District. A writer in *Country Life* in 1974 described how a stretch of road in this part of northern Staffordshire:

> '. . . has been well known to be haunted by a big black dog. Many years ago, my grandfather came home in a state of shock, after encountering the phantom one night. My aunt, not an imaginative woman, told me she had once felt something sniff at her hand when she was walking home one evening, but on turning round saw nothing to account for the sensation.'

A phantom black dog is said to be seen at the lane end near haunted Hermitage Farm, at Ipstones near Leek; another is said to appear at Indefont Well in the same village. In the moorlands his chief attribute appears to be guarding wayside graves. The retreat of Bonnie Prince Charlie's Highland army from Derby through the area in 1745 appears to have left in its wake a crop of stories of this kind; at Swinscoe on the Leek-Ashbourne road, three Jacobites were ambushed, and a ghostly black dog is said to guard their graves. At Bradnop, near Leek, a black dog haunts the road behind Oxhay Farm, where another Jacobite was treacherously slain by a companion.

Another haunted skull, whose story has been overshadowed by that of Dickey O'Tunstead, is preserved to this day at Flagg Hall, near Buxton, in an incongruous position on a cheeseboard in a window-sill on the staircase. According to this story, the skull – whose origin is

Flagg Hall, near Buxton, home of a 'screaming skull'

again unknown – reputedly refuses to be moved, and has remained in its chosen home for many hundreds of years despite change of ownership of the hall. The Flagg Hall skull is recorded as far back as the eighteenth century, when William Burdekin lived there. A distant relative of the Burdekin family recalls how she was told that:

> . . . they found an old skull in the house and were going to re-bury it in Chelmorton churchyard. They all piled into the trap and set off, or rather they didn't, as the horse refused to move, no matter how it was coaxed or shouted at. So they all got down and went back into the house. Then the horse walked calmly back to the stable. The skull was taken back up to the attic and peace reigned for a time. Then a new servant arrived and was given the attic bedroom; she took against the skull and flung it through the window. It landed on top of a cart-load of manure just going to the field. The horse stopped in its tracks, then kicked and reared and made such fuss, that the skull fell off onto the road. It was left outside for a time, but such ill-luck and misfortune befell the farm that it was taken back into the farm . . .

Hope Valley and District

Hope Valley ghosts and legends

The view from Moorseats over Hathersage village, far below, and at some distance, is surely one of the loveliest in England. I first beheld it on September 7th, 1954, entering the occasion in my diary, since it was on the one resplendent day we had throughout a summer and autumn of persistent rain . . . it instantly recalled the exquisite sense of the English countryside one finds in such poets as A. E. Housman. Derbyshire might well have been one of his 'coloured counties'.

So wrote Alastair Alpin McGregor in *The Ghost Book,* published in 1955. His viewpoint was from historic Moorseats Hall, on the hillside above Hathersage Church in the picturesque Hope Valley. Part of the hall has been dated as belonging to the thirteenth century, and three small windows on the south wall are oddly positioned, suggesting the presence of an older room unconnected with the modern house. There have been suggestions that part of the house was once the cell of a monk or a small chapel. Whatever the case, Moorseats is traditionally known as the house where, in the epic novel *Jane Eyre,* the heroine sheltered from a snowstorm, for Charlotte Brontë once visited Hathersage in order to absorb its 'atmosphere'. The house on the hillside is haunted by a 'white lady' ghost, who walks the garden beneath the yew trees through an orchard. The ghost is unique locally as it is said to appear in the form of somebody living in the house at the time of its manifestation.

The most prominent of the ancient families of the Hope Valley were the Eyres, who are said to have arrived in England with William the Conqueror. Granted land in the valley after the Conquest, they married well and eventually came to own most of the big houses in the region. In the time of Henry III it was recorded that William Le Eyr held land at Hope and the Forest of the High Peak, and his descendant Nicholas Eyre is said to have led a detachment of local men to fight at the Battle of Agincourt. Nicholas was the father of Robert Eyre, of Highlow Hall, an ancient manor house hidden in a fold of hills

Hope Dale, seen from the Winnats Pass at Castleton

Highlow Hall, Hathersage – 'reputedly the most haunted house in Derbyshire'

south-west of Hathersage. A persistent legend associated with Robert from an early date tells how he built a hall for each of his seven sons, all of them within sight of one another so they could keep in touch by using a signalling system.

Another legend accuses Robert, or his father Nicholas, of the cold-blooded murder of a workman whom he caught loitering on the job. In some versions of the story it is said that the murderer built the church at Hathersage in expiation of his sins, but this story must be false as the church was built at least a century before either of the two men was born. However, the ghost of the workman is said to haunt the premises, along with two female ghosts, one of whom, the White Lady of Highlow Hall, has been seen by many independent witnesses over the years.

Highlow Hall has been described by Roy Christian as 'reputedly the most haunted house in Derbyshire', and its ghosts have attracted so much attention that on one occasion television cameras were installed in an attempt to capture the paranormal visitors on film. The first record of a haunting at the hall is from as far back as the fourteenth century, when it is said that the scheming Nicholas Eyre wooed two sisters of the Archer family, to claim their inheritance; when the elder sister discovered the truth she fled the hall and was never seen alive again. Shortly afterward, her ghost is said to have appeared to Nicholas, gliding down the great oak staircase to confront him in the banqueting hall, where she laid a curse on the Eyre family. Despite the Eyres' earlier strength, the curse appears to have worked, as by the early nineteenth century the hall had passed out of the family, whose lands and titles diminished.

The 'white lady' is said to be the ghost of a lady murdered in an upstairs bedroom, from which her body was dragged along the landing and down the oak staircase. Ghost-hunter A. A. McGregor described the interior of the hall as 'one of the weirdest and most eerie I have ever examined', and during his visit in the 1950s he established that 'belief in the phantom of a white lady haunting the house is firmly established in the district. No one questions its existence'. One of the stories he was able to investigate occurred in 1911 and involved a carter from Dronfield. He had been delivering a load to the village of Abney, and was returning home past the hall at two o'clock in the morning when he saw a lady dressed in white in the yard; she was standing with the palms of her hands resting on the cattle trough, staring into the water. A farmer living nearby told how he often saw the ghost on moonlit nights, crossing the old courtyard seemingly oblivious to his presence, even when he touched his cap and uttered the greeting 'Goodnight, missus'.

When Roy Christian visited Highlow in 1969 to research an article for *Derbyshire Life,* he was told by the owners that they had not seen the ghost but had heard strange noises in the night, and that a lady visitor to the hall had reported seeing the ghostly figure of a man. No one in recent years, however, appears to have seen the spectre of a man 'dressed in white, and riding a white horse, which appears at midnight', described by S. O. Addy in his book on Derbyshire folklore published in 1895. Perhaps this was the ghost of one of the Eyres, visiting their Peakland home on a favourite steed?

Another 'white lady' haunts the vicarage at Hathersage Church, and was seen earlier this century by the Revd Brooksbank, who was also a respected local historian. It is said that one of the doors in the building is opened by the ghost every year on a certain night, 28 February.

The church in the historic village of Hathersage (written 'Hereseige' in 1086) is dedicated to the dragon-slaying St Michael, and stands on a hilltop which was probably sacred before the arrival of the first Christian missionaries in the Hope Valley. To the east of the churchyard is an earthwork known as Camp Green, or the Danes Camp, of uncertain date. In the churchyard is a stone pillar known as the 'sun stone', which was the centre of a strange ceremony as recently as the eighteenth century. Until then 'all bodies brought into the churchyard were carried around the sun-stone three times the way the sun went, this was for perfection'. This was no doubt a relic of sun worship in pagan times, as St Michael was a saint often invoked in areas where strong pagan cults resisted the first missionaries.

Lingering beliefs of ancient origin explain many other superstitions in this region. For example, in the past the dead were buried only in the south side of the churchyards at Hathersage, Hope and Castleton, as the north side was believed to be unlucky. At Hathersage, the inhabitants of Bamford and Derwent villages were buried in the north of the churchyard, whilst at Castleton the residents of Edale were obliged to come to church for Whitsunday communion, but were not allowed to enter except by way of a little path on the north side of the graveyard, and through the 'Devil's Door'. This door was always on the north wall of the church. At Hope, until recently, bridal couples entered and left the church only by way of the Devil's Door, and never by the fourteenth-century south porch. It was firmly believed that if this custom was not followed, the couples would meet some misfortune shortly afterwards; one local woman maintained that two brides she knew died shortly after the wedding as a consequence of breaking the custom.

St Peter's Church, Hope

St Peter's Church at Hope is the oldest recorded Christian place of worship in the northern Peak District, and in Saxon times it was the focus of one of the largest parishes in England, stretching from the Derwent woodlands in the north to Buxton, Tideswell and the Padley gorge. The Domesday Book mentions a church and a priest at Hope, and the present church, although dating mainly from the fourteenth century, contains within its stone fabric many traces of earlier beliefs. The north wall of the church features some of the finest gargoyles in the north of England: human faces, mouth-pullers, a clear phallic image and two representations of the horned god of the Celts. Histories and descriptions of the church and its architecture fail to mention these blatant pagan symbols, although they are plainly visible to visitors who know what they are looking for.

In 1881 the chancel, which was undoubtedly the oldest part of the church, was pulled down and rebuilt, and during the work two ancient tomb slabs were unearthed, lying in the foundations, upon which the walls had been built. The slabs were carved with pictures of crosses and forestry implements. 'So fresh and perfect is the work', noted a report at the time, 'that the squaring lines by which the mason guided himself in making out the design may still be seen'. The designs suggested that these were the graves of two officials of the Royal Forest of the Peak, which included Hope woodlands. The presence of the graves in the church suggested to antiquarians at the time that 'early in the thirteenth century the builders of this chancel so far paid deference to the ancient heathen rite as to prepare gravestones and pretend to bury human beings under the north and south walls'.

The church itself lies only a short distance across the fields from the ruins of the Roman fort at Brough, near Bradwell, which may be the castle or 'burgh' recorded at Hope during the reign of Edward I. Brough was known to the Romans as 'Anavio', and a road ran from here to the sacred spring at Buxton, and another across the high moors, linking the military garrison at Melandra, near Glossop, with the fort at Templeborough, near Rotherham, now obliterated by the steelworks. The fort was excavated in 1904, and again in recent years by local archaeologists, who have discovered coins, an underground strong-room and many inscribed stones.

Across the road, directly opposite the grassy bank which is all that remains of the fort today, is the Travellers Rest public house – the home of the ghost of a woman dressed in black. The legend runs that the spectre is that of a young woman, who died falling down a spiral staircase whilst escaping from a drunken labourer one Christmas eve, many hundreds of years ago. Rumour has it that the ghost glides along an upstairs corridor of the inn each Christmas eve, holding a bunch of keys in her hand. In 1974, the landlord Con Sullivan, an Army veteran, admitted to a local newspaper that he had 'a feeling that something is going on here. There is a "presence" all the time, and it frightens me'.

The legend of Robin Hood and Little John of Hathersage

Many visitors to the Hope Valley today are attracted by the area's romantic connections with the legendary outlaw Robin Hood, and more specifically with Little John, his faithful companion. The focal point for the legend has always been Hathersage, where to this day what is said to be the final resting place of the famous giant can be seen to the north-west of the churchyard. As early as 1686 it was described as 'the grave where they say Little John was buried, which is 14 foot in length'.

The facts behind the legend will probably never be known, but what seems certain is that the very earliest versions of the legend connect the activities of Robin Hood with the Forest of Barnsdale, in South Yorkshire, rather than with the more popularly known Sherwood Forest. In the seventeenth century Roger Dodsworth wrote that:

> Robin Locksley was born at Bradfield parish in Hallamshire, wounded his stepfather to death at plough, fled into the woods, and was relieved by his mother until discovered. Then he went to Clifton-upon-Calder, and became acquainted with Little John who kept the kine, which said John is buried at Hathershead [Hathersage] in Derbyshire, where he hath a fair tombstone, with an inscription.

This statement may support the legend that Robin Hood himself was born in the village of Loxley, eight miles to the north of Hathersage, now swallowed up by the suburbs of the city of Sheffield. A survey of the estate of the Earl of Arundel in 1637 records how at Loxley there was 'Little Haggas Croft [pasture] wherein is ye foundacion of an house or Cottage where Robin Hood was borne; this piece is compassed about with Loxley firth [forest]'; also mentioned is 'Robin Hood's Bower', known from later church records to be a booth or tent. This was the setting for a May Day ceremony in which a man representing 'Robin Hood', or the Green Man, was dressed in a garland of leaves and flowers, a custom which survives at Castleton to the present day, in the form of the famous Garland Day.

The legend of Robin Hood reaches back into the mists of time, and the years have made it difficult to distinguish fact from fantasy. What does seem certain is that a man of enormous size was buried in the graveyard at Hathersage in days gone by. As far back as 1625, when the antiquarian Elias Ashmole visited the church, he recorded the strong local tradition and saw Little John's longbow hanging in the church alongside the monument to the Eyre family; Little John's green forester's cap was also once preserved in the church, as well as his arrows and some chain-mail. In the church porch today a medieval stone, said to be from the original grave, can be seen, clearly marked 'J.L.' (John Little), but the great longbow is absent, having been moved to Canon Hall, near Barnsley, in the eighteenth century. The bow was over six feet long, made of spliced yew, and required a pull of 160lbs to draw it.

Another story concerns the giant's grave itself. Legend describes how Little John buried his friend Robin at Kirklees Park in West Yorkshire, 'after which he sought out his native village, where he wished to lay his own bones. As he approached the Vale of Hathersage, it is said he remarked that his career would soon be ended, and shortly after he breathed his last'. It is believed he died in a small cottage which once stood to the east of the church, and was buried in the grave now in the care of the Ancient Order of Foresters, sheltered by ancient yew trees.

The Little John legend refused to die, and in 1784, Captain James Shuttleworth, a cousin of the Stanhopes of Canon Hall, opened the grave and unearthed a gigantic human thigh bone thirty inches

Little John's gravestone

(almost one metre) in length, indicating a man of huge stature. The bone was carried into Little John's Cottage, then still standing on the east side of the churchyard and the home of a Mr Shard, where it was measured on his tailor's board. The story goes that an old huntsman, seeing the bone, shook his head and warned 'No good will come to either of ye, so long as ye keep dead man's bones above ground!' And sure enough, after the bone had been removed, both Captain Shuttleworth and his cousin suffered from a series of misfortunes, including a hunting accident, until finally they persuaded the parish clerk to re-bury the bone in its grave.

In 1847 Dr Spencer Hall visited Hathersage and found Little John's Cottage still standing, and the tradition of his burial in the churchyard remaining strong. The cottage was then occupied by Jenny Shard, aged seventy years; she recalled how, as a child, she witnessed the opening of the grave, and the bone being measured by her father who had died in 1827, aged ninety years. He told her that Little John had died in the cottage where they lived, before he was laid to rest in the churchyard of the village he loved so much.

Little John's Cottage, Hathersage, c.1847

Many places on the border between Derbyshire and South Yorkshire bear the names of the legendary outlaws Robin Hood and Little John – wells, stones, public houses and even a hamlet – on East Moor between Baslow and Chesterfield. Unfortunately for those who believe that Robin was a real historical character, the majority of these names were recorded for the first time in the nineteenth century, when it was fashionable to name landscape features after the outlaw, in the same way that many prehistoric sites were habitually associated with and named after the druids at this time.

Robin Hood's Cave – one of the famous outlaw's many hiding places in Peakland

On Stanage Edge, the impressive gritstone edge which forms the border between Derbyshire and Yorkshire, a series of interconnecting caves and passages are known as 'Robin Hood's Cave', where, according to folklore, Robin once sheltered. Emerging from the opening of the cave half way down the face of the edge, the visitor is treated to panoramic views of the undulating vales and hills to the west, with Little John's resting place in the churchyard at Hathersage nestling in the valley below.

On the opposite side of the hills, on Offerton Moor near the hamlet of Shatton, is a stone pillar known as 'Robin Hood's Stoop', from which it is said that Robin fired an arrow across the valley to Hathersage Church, a distance of a mile and a half! The same hillside on Bradwell Edge in the parish of Hazelbadge conceals Robin Hood's Cross, described as 'Robins Crosse' in a document of the year 1319. This early date may provide evidence of the historical connections of the region with a real Robin Hood, but we know that the name was very popular in the Middle Ages and historians who have investigated the legend have discovered evidence of many other Robin Hoods scattered through history. Some of these characters – including a Thomas Robynhood recorded in document of 1388 – may have derived their names from having acted the part of 'Robin Hood', or the Green Man, in the May Games.

The words 'Robin', 'Robert' and 'Hood' are common in the field names of this part of the Peak District; in Hathersage itself, the Hood Brook runs past the cricket pitch and through the village. Near the Derwent Dams is a moor with the name 'Robin Hood's Moss'; and in the Longshaw Estate, near Fox House, there are two wells bearing the names Robin Hood and Little John.

Legends of Bradwell and Castleton
The ruined Catholic chapel at North Lees, on the hillside above Hathersage, was built in the time of Henry I, and was known as the Chapel of Holy Trinity, a dedication often associated with centres of well-worship. Close by the chapel was Holy Trinity Well, a sacred spring from time immemorial. John Wilson, a local antiquary, writing in 1780, described how:

> . . . there is a well near North Lees in Derbyshire near the remains of a Popish chapel to which ye papists resort one day in ye year early in the morning and every person puts in a pin, which custom was kept up a few years ago as I was told by the Rev. Mr Hadfield, Vicar of Hathersage, and I believe is still resorted to.

The pins were offered to the spirit or lady of the well in order to secure good luck and healing, and in the hope of clean water in the future. Elsewhere in the valley, at Bradwell and Castleton, there was once a belief that if children did not put pins into the local wells on Palm Sunday, 'they would break their bottles at Easter and the Lady of the Well would not let them have any clean water'. Local writer Seth Evans describes how from his childhood he remembered 'depositing a pin in a well in New Road, Bradwell, and finding whole handfuls of pins in the sand at the bottom of the well, the deposits of the village children for many generations'. Mr Robert Bradwell, aged eighty-eight, testified earlier this century that on Palm Sunday the children of the village 'used to put new pins into the lady wells and that the lady of the well would not let them have clean water until they did that'. Mr Bradwell said the object of the children was to get clean water 'by the lady's influence'.

The pins – 'which must be new and straight, not crooked' – placed in wells were symbols of fertility, often linked with offerings at holy wells. Pins and brooches of Romano-British date were found during excavations in Poole's Cavern, near Buxton – another centre of water worship – demonstrating the ancient origins of the belief in the miraculous healing power of wells. Dewric Well, on the hillside at Bretton above Eyam, was resorted to by barren women, as it was said to promote fertility in those who used its water. At Little Hucklow children used to climb onto the hillside on the morning of Palm Sunday to place a ring of 'palm' or pussy-willow around the Silver Well on Abney Moor. On Easter Sunday or Monday they also dropped pins into the same well and poured water on mixtures of broken sweets in bottles. This practice, known as 'Sugar-cupping' or 'Shak-bottle', was a popular Easter custom in many Peakland villages, including Castleton, Tideswell and Chapel-en-le-Frith. Here the children took sugar, sweets and liquorice to dissolve in the water of the local wells.

It will come as no surprise that belief in spirits and fairies dwelling in watery places gave rise to stories of ghosts and boggarts, one of whom, 'Jenny Greenteeth', may have been spread by anxious parents who wished to keep their children away from pools and boggy places. Bradwell's best-known ghost story is the tale of the 'Lumb Boggart' – according to the village historian Seth Evans, 'an absurd tale which everybody believed even down to half a century ago'. Even he had to admit that in his childhood he had 'crouched and run past "The Lumb" on a dark night, and oftener still has the hair on many heads stood straight when passing "Lumbley Pool" between Brough and Bamford'.

The story of the Lumb Boggart is said to originate in 1760, when the body of a young girl was discovered buried under the staircase of a house at Hillhead in the village. It was believed that the girl had been murdered, and soon her ghost began to make nightly appearances, scaring everyone in the neighbourhood. Driven to the end of their tether by the boggart, the villagers enlisted help from a warlock, who agreed to undertake the fearful task of 'laying' the ghost. The would-be exorcist arrived at the haunted house, and, surrounded by crowds of onlookers, chalked a ring on the chamber floor and fell to his knees in prayer, sweat pouring from his face. The spectators declared afterwards that they 'felt the floor move for yards up and down in quick succession', whereupon the magician exclaimed 'Arise! Arise! I command thee!' The spirit manifested itself and was ordered to depart and assume the body of a fish, and to locate itself in the Lumb Mouth, adding that every Christmas eve the ghost should assume the form of a white ousel, and fly to lonely Lumbley Pool.

The tiny hamlet of Shatton, on the hillside between Hathersage and Bradwell, has a haunted barn and a stile patrolled by a boggart, which once appeared to a local man at two stone stoops on Shatton Lane. 'It wasn't a dog or a ram', he said afterwards, 'Oh dear, no! It was something terrifying and supernatural'. These and many other ghost stories of the locality were recorded earlier this century by Dr Mary Andrews, a resident of Shatton, who collected stories of phantom horses, black dogs and hobgoblins. She told a writer in 1955 how 'people living in our isolated villages and on our lonely farms not only believe in them, but see and hear them!'

Hazelbadge Hall, Bradwell

Nearby Bradwell Dale is haunted by the ghost of Margaret Vernon, the last of the line of the Vernon family of Haddon Hall, one branch of whom lived at Hazelbadge Hall in the valley for three centuries. In Tudor times, so the legend runs, Margaret is said to have given herself in marriage to a man who had, unbeknown to her, plighted his troth with another, and when she discovered his treachery she rushed blindly to witness his marriage at Hope Church. On wild nights, when the winds howl furiously, and the rain falls in torrents, so they say, the ghost of a lady on horseback can be seen in the gorge between Bradwell and Hazelbadge 'rushing madly in the direction of the old Hall'.

There is a strong tradition in this part of the Hope Valley that the residents of Bradwell were originally descended from slaves, brought by the Romans from Gaul and Italy to work in the lead mines which were so important to the British economy at the time. From the Dark Ages, there are legends of great battles between the Anglo-Saxon warriors who were then arriving in the area. The Hope Valley is dominated by the twin peaks of Lose Hill and Win Hill, the latter resembling an extinct volcano from certain viewpoints. Tradition associates the names with a battle between Edwin, King of Northumbria, and a pagan King of Mercia, in the seventh century AD – the victors of the battle are said to have camped on the peak which later became Win Hill. Also at Bradwell is Edden Tree Farm, the place where a king or chieftain named Edwin was captured after a battle, and ritually hung from a tree. The famous Garland Ceremony at Castleton (see page 97) nearby may be a survival of an ancient fertility rite involving just such a death by ritual hanging.

In his book *Britannia,* written in 1586, William Camden describes the village of Castleton:

Near unto this Burgh (Brough) there standeth upon the top of a hill an old castle, sometimes belonging to the Peverels, called The Castle in the Peake, which King Edward III together with a Manour and an Honour gave to his sonne John, Duke of Lancaster. Under which there is a cave or hole within the ground, called saving your reverence, The Devil's Arse, that gapeth with a wide mouth, and hath in it many turnings, and relying rooms. Notwithstanding, by reason of these and such like fables, this Hole is reckoned for one of the wonders of England . . .

The 'Devil's Arse' is today more familiar to tourists as Peak Cavern; in an earlier superstitious age the limestone caves of Derbyshire were the abode of evil spirits. After heavy rain, when water ran from caves such as Treak Cliff, it was said that this was the Devil urinating. Another legend, recorded by Gervase of Tilbury in the twelfth century, concerns a young shepherd who strayed one winter's day into the entrance of the Peak Cavern whilst searching for a lost sow. Entering the cavern mouth he saw a light and concluded that the animal must have strayed inside. Walking further into the darkness he emerged into 'a very wide and large country with Rivulets and Brookes running here and there through it, and huge Pooles of dead and standing water'. In this strange new land, reapers were gathering in the harvest. Finding the lost sow and its litter, the shepherd returned safely to the mouth of the cavern, where he found to his astonishment that it was still winter in Derbyshire!

Winnats Pass, Castleton, haunted by a murdered couple

Another story concerns the famous Winnats Pass, a name originally written as 'Wyndeyates', or 'the pass through which the wind sweeps'. This is a limestone gorge through which the main road to Chapel-en-le-Frith now runs, since the new road by Mam Tor was blocked by a landslide. The gorge takes on an eerie atmosphere at night when the wind is howling; it is haunted by the ghosts of a young couple, Henry and Clara, who were murdered there in 1758. The historical accuracy of the story is questionable, but the tale runs that a young well-to-do couple were eloping to be married at the church in Peak Forest, and stopped at a Castleton inn to rest their horses. It was here that they were spotted by a group of lead-miners who, on the assumption that they were carrying valuables, plotted to ambush the couple later that night. On their way through the Winnats gorge, the young lovers were attacked by five ruffians, and horribly put to death, their bodies buried near a barn in which they had been robbed.

In one version of the story it is said that Clara had received a premonition of her own death in a dream, in which the ghost of her dead brother had appeared to her. Whatever the truth of the matter, the murderers were never brought to human justice, though it is said that they all received their just rewards through a supernatural power – one of them being killed by a rockfall, another went mad, and a third hanged himself. Many years later, the skeletons of the two young lovers were unearthed by miners sinking an engine-shaft in Winnats, and hastily re-buried in the churchyard at Castleton. The pass thereafter took on an eerie reputation in local lore, and it is said today that the ghosts of the murdered couple still appear, begging for mercy when the wind is howling through the gorge.

Castle Hotel, Castleton, home to four ghosts

Castleton today is a crowded target of tourist attention, with its show caverns and souvenir shops selling trinkets made from local minerals, most famous of which is the banded fluorspar known as Blue John. In the heart of the village is the Castle Hotel, one of the best-known haunted houses in the Peak District. The building boasts no fewer than four possible ghosts, including that of a jilted bride, a lady in grey and a middle-aged phantom in a pin-striped suit! The small, elderly woman dressed in grey may have the oldest pedigree of the spirits in the bar, although little seems to be known about her today; she was last reported by a local councillor, who saw a small elderly woman in a grey dress, standing by the door in the main bar. As he moved towards her, she vanished.

The upstairs corridor of the hotel is the haunt of the jilted bride, who glides around in a white gown with a veil. The last person to see her was a chambermaid, who immediately rushed downstairs screaming. Yet another female ghost was reported in the spring of 1962, when the new landlord and a friend were reported to have seen the misty figure of a woman walking along the corridor, with her legs and feet curiously positioned on an earlier level below the present floorboards!

The unusual appearance of this spectre is perhaps explained by the many structural alterations which have altered the appearance of the hotel over the centuries. Dr Mary Andrews was told by a young mason of the discovery of a Roman coin in the building during repairs, as well as a walled-up fireplace; there is also a gruesome story about a woman who was murdered and buried under the doorstep in 1603. Such an event may explain the persistent stories of hauntings by female ghosts, but on Hallowe'en night 1960 (the traditional time of year for the appearance of spirits), landlord Philip Williams reported seeing a strange man standing by the frosted glass window in the tap room. The figure was a gentleman in his sixties, with greying hair, dressed in a pin-striped suit. Mr Williams said at the time that:

> I had never seen him before and when I spoke he vanished. It may sound far-fetched, but the man was there one minute and gone the next. My wife knew something was up when she saw my pale face, and my heart was thumping like a drum.

Another haunted building in Castleton is Goosehill Hall, the residence of another 'grey lady' whose exploits have been overshadowed by her colleague at the Castle Hotel! Mary Andrews writes that the hall was the residence in the 1920s of a couple who claimed to possess psychic powers. They not only saw the ghost, but also a phantom re-enactment of a great medieval tournament on Castle Hill, which folklore says involved an English prince and a king of Scotland.

Peveril Castle and Cave Dale

Peveril Castle was immortalised in Sir Walter Scott's novel *Peveril of the Peak,* published in 1823. The ruinous keep and gateway are of twelfth century date, but the castle, the only surviving example of any real importance in the Peak District, was built in the time of William Peveril, William the Conqueror's bailiff in Peakland. Castle Hill towers above the village, with Peak Cavern and Cave Dale below and the 'Shivering Mountain' of Mam Tor in the distance. Mam Tor is crowned by defensive earthworks dating from the late Bronze Age, and the name is thought to preserve the name of a Celtic mother goddess, whose great stronghold once dominated the Hope Valley. The castle became the centrepoint of the Norman village which was created in the early Middle Ages. The small chapel which later became St Edmund's Church was probably the work of the same masons who built the fortress on the hill which it served.

The site of Castle Hill was important before the arrival of the Norman lords, for it is believed that the Druids worshipped on the hill, and folklore tells how Castleton people would climb the hill on Easter Sunday at six o'clock in the morning, to see the sun rise above the mountains, for 'on this day the sun is said to dance for joy at his rising'. On the same day they would also pay pilgrimage to Russett Well, an underground spring which emerges at the mouth of Peak Cavern, with the water drunk in a ritual survival of sun-worship. In pagan times the well was sacred, with the nearby cavern a symbolic entrance to the Otherworld.

In 1976 a carving of a human face on a block of limestone was unearthed in the garden of Waterside Cottage, by Russett Well. The stone cult head is carved in a tradition which stretches back to the Celtic Iron Age, and one authority has noted that it has a purposefully winking eye, resembling depictions of one-eyed gods found in Irish mythology. The pagan head cult was often associated with springs and wells, and a short distance away, in the shadow of Mam Tor, lies Dunscar Farm, where for many years a human skull was preserved, which was kept on the outside of a window-sill; it was said that 'if it is removed, the crops fare badly'. Where the skull is today, no one knows.

Paganism survives in Castleton in the form of the world-famous Garland Day, which takes place annually on Oak Apple Day, usually 29 May, unless this falls on a Sunday. The Garland is a very important date for the villagers; on the evening before, they assemble at the church to fasten branches of oak, elm and sycamore to the church tower. The following morning, a beehive-shaped frame of wood is constructed and throughout the morning is decorated with flowers and foliage gathered from the surrounding countryside. The Garland is topped by the 'queen', a small oak posy covered with flowers which is now placed upon the war memorial before the end of the ceremony.

The procession begins around six o'clock in the evening, when the Garland King (or Green Man) and his female consort, the Queen, are paraded around the village, accompanied by Morris dancers, local children and the Castleton Silver Band, which performs a traditional tune unique to the village, known as *Pudding in a Lantern*:

Ah dunna know, Ah dunna care,
*   What they do i' Bradda:*
Piece o' beef an' a owd cow's yeead,
*   An' a puddin' baked i' a lantern.*

Does the last line of the verse, as some suggest, refer to a sacrifice which the primitive-looking Garland originally symbolised? The strange procession ends when the Garland is hoisted to the centre pinnacle of the church tower (the church is dedicated to the Anglo-Saxon king, St Edmund the Martyr), where it remains until it decays.

It is recorded that many years ago, one of the vicars caused a great stir when he cast down the Garland from the church tower because he felt that the tradition was pagan, and rooted in the sacrificial rites of the Druids. Previous to this occasion, however, the church had encouraged the annual ceremony, as the earliest recorded mention of it occurs in the parish registers, where an entry for 1749 reads: 'Paid for an iron rod to hang up ye ringers garland . . . £0.0.8d'.

The association of the Garland Day with the Stuart period (today the King and Queen wear Stuart costumes) came in the seventeenth century, when the festival became linked with the escape of King Charles II from the Parliamentary forces after the Battle of Worcester. Until 1955 the part of the Garland Queen was played by a man dressed as a woman, who 'was given to making coarse remarks'; the King and Queen were accompanied by uniformed outriders, as well as by men sweeping the road with besoms to allow the procession to move along the crowded streets. These details suggest the ceremony existed before the Civil War, and some scholars believe that the horseman represents the Green Man or Jack-in-the Green, often portrayed in medieval art as a grotesque head with branches and greenery spewing from his mouth.

Garland Day is a survival of a pagan summer festival signifying the rebirth of nature after the winter, a time when, even in the twentieth century, residents of Castleton return home from every corner of the world to take part in the festivities. It is not surprising that locally the Garland is known as Castleton's 'baby night'; one old character was overhead remarking to another 'Ee were getten on Garland Neet, and tha mun work that out for theesen'.

Edale and the northern moors

Edale village, nestling in a green valley beneath a background of high moors, is today a focal point for tourists, and a magnet for walkers arriving at the southern starting-point of the notorious 250-mile-long Pennine Way. In the past, Edale was a tiny hamlet hidden in a lonely cul-de-sac, cut off from the neighbouring villages of Castleton and Hope by the winter snows, until the arrival of the main Sheffield to Manchester railway line in the 1890s. The remote and inhospitable nature of the region is demonstrated by the local records, which describe how in 1711 a woman was frozen to death at Edale end, and earlier two men were buried for months in snow on Win Hill; whilst March 1716 'saw a most severe snowing and driving that hath been seen in the memory of man in the High Peak'.

In medieval times the village consisted of a number of small hamlets, made up of houses clustered around farm buildings, known locally as 'booths', enclosed to keep out the wolves which still roamed the hills. There are no wolves today, but the valley is the haunt of a phantom black dog, which has been reported at several locations, most notably between Upper Booth and Barber Booth. The dog stalks the 'Tips', a name for the heaps of earth and stone exacavated from the hillside during the construction of the Cowburn railway tunnel. Peakland residents are said to avoid this area after dusk, in fear of meeting the ghost-hound.

In 1930, one evening at eight o'clock, Greta Shirt of Crowdenlea at Edale was returning home along a lonely lane between Upper Booth and the Lea, when she clearly saw in the rays of the moon what she took to be a black dog 'the size of a very large black collie'. She wondered whose dog it was, and as it passed by her side, she put her hand down to stroke it, but found herself unable to do so. Without warning the dog 'merged through the close, criss-cross wires of the fence, which could not possibly have let its body through'. Instantly, she looked over the fence, but could see no trace of the dog, and on reaching home told her father what she had seen. 'Well, now that you've seen it', Farmer Shirt observed, 'I'll admit there is a black dog ghost along there; but I did not tell you until you were grown out of your childhood'. He also admitted to having seen it himself some years previously, in the same location.

A more fearsome animal terrorised the valley earlier this century, when in October 1925 the *Daily Express* described how the Edale district was alarmed by a creature 'of enormous size, black in colour and possessing a howl like a fog-horn', which hid in an unknown lair during the daytime, and at night roamed the countryside baying horribly. The creature, whose description is reminiscent of the 'Hound of the Baskervilles' in Sir Arthur Conan Doyle's famous story, was said to have killed dozens of sheep in the space of one night, leaving their carcasses strewn about, with legs, shoulders and heads torn off. It was said that 'people in many places are so frightened that they refuse to leave their homes after dusk, and keep their children in the house'. Posses of farmers set out onto the hills, armed with rifles in an attempt to hunt down the creature, but had no success in solving the mystery.

Stories about strange animals which live on the remote moors of the High Peak have continued to the present day. As recently as November 1989, armed policemen searched lonely Ollersett Moor, between Hayfield and New Mills, after a farmer and a police patrol spotted 'a large black panther'. A police spokesman at the time said:

> It was seen by unarmed officers but, obviously, they did not get too close. By the time we had got ourselves geared up with armed officers, it had gone. From what we can gather from the experts, it is a leopard-type animal.

Maybe this was the same ghostly creature spotted on the B6049 road which links Miller's Dale with the A6 north-east of Buxton. Local folklore describes how motorists have been pursued here by a strange wolf-like animal which runs and leaps at immense speed, pursuing cars at night. The village of Wormhill nearby is the place where the last wolf in England was killed in the sixteenth century, a fact which perhaps lies behind the local stories of ghostly hounds.

Typical of the ghostlore of this region is a story in *Derbyshire Life* (December 1964) which describes how one winter's day a man went into a public house in a lonely part of the hills of the High Peak. The bar was deserted except for a large black and white collie dog lounging by the fire. After the man had called to the dog without a response, a farmer entered the bar and the landlord emerged to serve his two customers. Shortly afterwards, when the visitor looked for the dog, he found it had vanished, and said to the other men 'That's funny, I didn't see the dog go out; he isn't very friendly, is he?' The farmer and the landlord looked at each other and asked 'What dog?' The visitor then described the dog to the two men, whereupon the farmer hastily drank his beer and hurried out. 'He's gone to fetch the sheep down off the hill to lower pastures', the landlord told the visitor. 'That dog always appears when there's going to be a bad snowfall.'

The story describes how the owner of the dog had been caught in a fierce blizzard whilst tending his flock of sheep on the hills, and his faithful hound – which stayed with him – had died shortly afterwards. Since the tragedy, the ghost of the dog appears just before a heavy snowfall as a warning to others who might meet the same fate.

Other weird experiences are reported from the dark lanes and eerie roads in this desolate region sandwiched between the conurbations of

Sheffield and Greater Manchester. Isolated farmhouses and inns harbour ghostly residents, best known of which is the 'grey lady' said to appear in the grounds of the Strines Inn, on the lonely Bradfield moors, west of Sheffield.

Strines Inn, Bradfield

Stories abound of 'white lady' ghosts, strange hovering lights and mysterious underground passages, but of special interest is the ghost reported by a Rotherham motorist, on the road from Bamford which crosses the famous Ladybower Reservoir, described by Roy Christian in *Ghosts and Legends*. Mr Grover was riding his motorbike towards the junction with the Snake road late one night when he spotted what appeared to be a horse and cart in the beam thrown by his headlight. Observing closer, he noted that the cart was of an unusual design, having high sides and back, with a strange driver who walked alongside the horse holding a long whip. As the motorcyclist pulled out to overtake he was momentarily dazzled by the undipped headlights of an approaching car. After recovering, he once again pulled out to overtake the horse and cart, but found to his astonishment that the road in front of him was deserted! 'Thinking that perhaps the horse had taken fright', said Mr Grover, 'I got off my [motorbike] and searched the side of the road, which there fell off rather steeply'; however, there was no sign of the strange cart or its driver, and no turnings from the road for nearly a mile.

The most puzzling legend from this region concerns a 'phantom hitch-hiker'. One winter's evening early in the 1960s, a young couple were riding a motorbike and sidecar along the moorland road which links Fox House, near Hathersage, with the city of Sheffield. They were flagged down by a girl in a leather jacket and crash-helmet, who asked for a lift to an address in the city. On their approach to the suburbs of Sheffield, the man realised his pillion-riding passenger had vanished, and despite returning to Fox House they were unable to find any trace of her. After reporting the strange incident to the police in Sheffield, the man and his girlfriend decided to check the address which the hitch-hiker had given him. The door of the house was answered by the girl's distraught mother, and it soon transpired that her daughter, whose description perfectly matched that of the hitch-hiker in the leather jacket, had been killed only a few days before in a motorcycle accident on that same stretch of road . . .

The High Peak District

Kinder Scout – mermaids, boggarts and white ladies

The village of Hayfield is dominated by the encircling rocky plateau of Kinder Scout – the highest mountain in the Peak District, a desolate wilderness of chocolate-brown peat groughs and spectacular eroded rock formations. 'Kinder' is an obscure name, of possible Celtic origin, although one antiquarian, S. O. Addy, related it directly to the Germanic 'kunder', meaning creature, being or prodigy; whereas Scout may be from 'skuti' or 'scoute', meaning a cave or rock formed by jutting rocks.

The prodigy in this case may be the legendary water nymph said to frequent an eerie expanse of water below Kinder Downfall. At the foot of the famous rock Downfall, where on rare occasions the River Kinder provides one of the few waterfalls in the region, lies the black

Kinder Scout

'. . . the mountain torrent of the Downfall where Kinder comes roaring down in
flood time through a steep stoney ravine . . .'

104

acidic mire shown on Ordnance Maps as the Mermaid's Pool, which takes on a sinister aspect when the sky above is heavily laden with snow or when a storm is raging. Ward, in *Highways and Byways of Derbyshire*, alludes to 'the mountain torrent of the Downfall where Kinder comes roaring down in flood time through a steep, stoney ravine, and the Mermaid's Pool where Jenny Crum was drowned, and to which the two children paid their midnight visit on Easter Eve...'

Many sinister stories are connected with this pool of lifeless marsh water; it is said that no animal will drink from it, and no fish can survive in its murky depths. Clarence Daniel described the pool as having 'an atmosphere of melancholy; a sense of desolation which suggests that some malign influence has cast its spell over the place'. Like the Ebbing and Flowing Well at Barmoor Clough, legend asserts that the Mermaid's Pool is connected with the distant Atlantic Ocean, perhaps due to the salty acidic nature of its water.

Whatever the case it is said that anyone who visits the pool on Easter eve will see the water spirit swimming in the magic pool and will either receive the gift of eternal life or will be dragged under the water to their death. Mythical water monsters are common in Celtic

Mermaid's Pool, Kinder Scout, home of a water spirit

folklore; for example, in Scotland there is the Water Horse, which haunted the lochs and lured children to their deaths in the slimy depths. Belief in the existence of the mermaid was once very strong in the Hayfield region, and it is said that locals regularly made pilgrimages to the lonely pool in the hope of seeing her. A frequent visitor to the pool was a soldier, Aaron Ashton, of Hayfield, who died in the year 1835 aged 104, despite the fact that he never saw the fabled Mermaid, or admitted the fact if he had.

Before the arrival of good roads and electricity, this region was wild and remote, with the stagecoach being the chief link with the outside world, when some of the present well-known roads were little more than pack-horse tracks across the treacherous moors. Before the beginning of the present century, the High Peak was a region of great isolation, and with the lack of all-weather access, the population of the moorland villages formed a close-knit and secretive community which preserved ancient traditions and archaic beliefs to the present day. In the 1940s, 'H.R.B.', of Coombs House, writing in a local newspaper, described how in this period the 'Kinder Boggart' roamed the wilds around the Downfall, striking terror into the heart of many a farmer and shepherd returning home at night:

> . . . then there was the 'Milking Hillock Ghost' making its presence known by the rattling of chains and 'Peggy with th'Lantern', swung its light on the summit of Lantern Pike on dark nights.

Strange and unaccountable sounds are heard among the lonely moors and hills of the Kinder Scout region. Once, a farmer and his son, walking home near South Head from sheep-shearing, heard several times a noise like 'the cry of some injured person soliciting help'. Further north, on the boggy moorland expanse of Bleaklow, strange lights and the clanking armour of ghostly Roman soldiers have been seen and heard. Hidden in a fold of the hills south-east of Hayfield is South Head Farm, the scene of a murder in the distant past of a woman by her jealous lover. The bloodcurdling sound of her corpse being dragged downstairs in the house has been heard by many visitors over the years, as well as a phantom splash as the body is flung into a pool at Stoney Ford, near where a pack-horse bridge carries the bridle-path to Hayfield across the River Noe. According to one version, the splash is always preceded by 'a prolonged and eerie scream as of a boy's being dragged down the field from Edale Head farmhouse, now in ruins, to be drowned in this field'.

Stoney Ford is overlooked by Edale Cross, an ancient boundary stone at the centre of the Royal Forest of the Peak, which marked the boundary of the land given to the Abbey of Basingwerk in 1157; the present stone carries the date of 1810, carved on the year of its re-erection by the local farmers. The Peaklanders of old were a superstitious race, and believed in the existence of all manner of supernatural omens and ghostly creatures. A. A. McGregor noted how old Farmer Bradbury, once resident at South Head Farm, was typical of others in the area, being strongly superstitious – never taking an even number of sheep to market, and never starting a new job or moving house on a Friday, or on the thirteenth day of a month.

Until recently, there existed a strong local tradition that a meadow between South Head Farm and Stoney Ford was haunted by the ghost of a lady in white, connected in some fashion with the shadowy murder at the farm. Early this century, a group of Irish labourers involved in hay-making in the meadow saw a ghostly 'girl in white' who glided across the fields down to the stream where she disappeared; they knew nothing of the local tradition at the time of their sighting, being casual labourers who had only just arrived in the district. Perhaps connected with this story is the name of a large standing stone on the Coldwell Clough Road, overlooking The Ashes Farm, which is called the 'White Lady'. On the face of the stone is a small hole which looks down upon the farm, and it is said that 'when viewed through this hole at night the farm is supposed to appear to move from side to side!', though perhaps alcoholic stimulation may be necessary before this display is complete!

Highgate Hall, between Coldwell Clough and the village of Hayfield, is the scene of the murder of a Scottish pedlar many hundreds of years ago. The unsolved murder took place near the site of a well, now sealed, and it is said that afterwards his ghost haunted the hall. At one time villagers were 'feared' to pass the hall after dark, because of the 'Thiggate Hall Ghost', as it became known. The bones of the victim were dug up and re-interred in Hayfield cemetery in 1770, and it is now said that as long as the well remains sealed, 'the ghost of the pedlar will not haunt the area'.

Hayfield Chapel itself has an odd ghost story, for it is recorded that in 1754 a fantastic happening occurred in the churchyard. Here, at the site of a communal grave of flood victims, in the presence of many witnesses:

Hayfield Church – scene of a fantastic happening in 1754

... on the last of August, several Hundreds of Bodies rose out of the Grave in the open day in that Church, to the great astonishment and Terror of several spectators. They deserted the Coffin, and rising out of the grave, immediately ascended directly towards Heaven, singing in Consert all along as they mounted thro' the Air; they had no winding sheets, about them, yet did not appear quite naked, their Vesture seem'd streak'd with gold, interlaced with sable, skirted with white, yet thought to be exceeding light by the agility of their motions, and the swiftness of their ascent. They left a most fragrant and delicious Odour behind them, but were quickly out of sight ...

This occurrence is recorded in a letter written to a colleague by the Revd Dr James Clegg, a down-to-earth non-conformist minister of religion from nearby Chapel-en-le-Frith.

Long Lee Farm, Rowarth, near Hayfield

An assortment of ghosts can be found at ancient Long Lee Farm, near Rowarth, once the home of the illustrious Hyde family (one of whom belonged to the Worshipful Company of Merchant Tailors of the City of London). Most notable of the ghosts said to inhabit the farmhouse is the 'White Lady of Long Lee', which passed through doors and walls 'with the greatest of ease', and which was reputedly the ghost of a miserly member of the family, whose death-bed was kept in the house for many years. Another gruesome relic of the past is the gravestone of John Hyde, which is preserved today in the structure of the cattle shippen of the farm. The gravestone was one of several which were washed away from the churchyard in Hayfield during a great flood in the mid-eighteenth century; legend has it that any attempt to remove the stone from its place of rest will result in disaster. The curse was tested some years ago when the stone was moved and it is said that shortly afterwards a power cable fell, electrocuting cattle in the adjacent farrowing-shed!

Many residents of Long Lee have over the years experienced unexplained happenings in the gaunt farmhouse. The Stacey family, who lived there before the present owners, were so perturbed by 'strange clankings' one night that the whole household sought refuge in the nearby Little Mill Inn, a building with a ghost of its own! In the late 1930s a visitor to the farm enquired of the maid there if she had seen anything of the ghost. She said she had not, but one night whilst she lay in bed, a banging noise had terrified her; however, on investigation, this had proved to be the long clock which stood on the landing and had tumbled downstairs!

Also part of the farm's ghostly repertoire is the 'Boggart Room', in reality a bedroom adjoining an eight-foot-thick interior wall, reputed to contain the coffin of a three-year old child. Local legend asserts that the child was buried in the house during the seventeenth century in order to avoid the Shroud Tax levied on burials in public churchyards at that time. Similar house-burials are known from other parts of the Peak District, and may originate in the pagan past when it was believed that no building would be secure until a living creature was interred in the foundations.

Not far away is another haunted house, Aspinshaw Hall, once the scene of violent disturbances which today would be classified as poltergeist phenomena. The strange happenings are said to have begun in the seventeenth century, after the death of a well-known lawyer who lived there. His relics objected to being moved, and any attempt to clear them from the house was followed by nightly disturbances, with bedclothes dragged from the bed and rumbling noises scaring the inmates by night. In the same area is Ringstones

Farm, whose name suggests it is the site of a lost prehistoric stone circle.

Cut off by high land from the rest of Derbyshire, the extreme north-west of the Peak District, near the Cheshire border, has the largest concentration of Celtic place-names in the whole region. Professor Cameron suggests that the area around Rowarth, where there is a cluster of seven Celtic names, 'was the area of the country settled latest in Anglo-Saxon times'. It comes as no surprise then, that this is also a region where the relics of old beliefs and superstitions have lingered from the remote past to the present day.

Ghosts and witches of Longdendale

The town of Glossop is sometimes called Howard Town, because so many of the buildings there were at one time either built or owned by the Catholic Howard family, the Dukes of Norfolk. When the line of the main Sheffield to Manchester railway reached the town in the 1840s it stimulated the cotton industry, and Glossop was transformed into a prosperous mill-town. Prior to this period, Glossop and the valley of Longdendale which it dominates had long been introverted and intensely localised in outlook. Despite its integration into the industrial conurbation of the West Riding, traces of past cultures were not obliterated, and each mill-town and village remained, almost to the present day, cut off from the others and largely isolated.

Old Glossop is the more ancient part of the town, where seventeenth-century houses cluster around the village green and cross. The former centre of village life is the parish church of All Saints, which was extensively rebuilt during the nineteenth and twentieth centuries. However, there was a church at Glossop mentioned in the Domesday Book, and this probably replaced an earlier wooden church of Saxon origin which stood on the site of a pagan temple. The manor of Glossop and its church were granted by King Henry II to the Abbey of Basingwerk in Flintshire in 1157, and for over three hundred years the Abbot was responsible for the appointment of vicars. The first vicar of which any record remains is a William, who in 1250 was charged in the court of the Royal Forest for hunting the King's deer with his bishop; the following year he was again fined for another hunting offence, along with his landlord, the Abbot! By the fifteenth century the manor was leased to the Earls of Shrewsbury, from whom it passed to the Howard family.

Nothing survives of the medieval church at Old Glossop other than a number of carved stone heads which survived, like many medieval

*All Saints Church, Glossop. The churchyard and vicarage are haunted by a
'grey lady'*

gargoyles, because of the existence of strong beliefs about their power to avert evil. Two of these carvings are now incorporated into the stone wall behind the new vicarage. Similar grotesque carvings of human heads and faces adorn the north wall and tower of the church at Mottram-in-Longdendale, to the west of Glossop. The church here, dedicated to St Michael & All Angels, stands on a prominent hilltop, no doubt the site of a pagan shrine before the arrival of Christianity in the region. The name 'Mottram' refers to a meeting-place or crossroads, and the hilltop on which the church stands is known as War Hill, after a fierce battle between warring English barons during the reign of King Stephen. It is said that the church, first recorded in the year 1250, was originally built as a memorial to those killed in the battle.

Another survival of the medieval period at Mottram was a custom whereby a huge mass of rushes and a number of garlands were carried round the town during Wakes week in August every year; finally, the garlands were given to the church wardens, who hung them from the roof of the church. In Glossop this custom survived until the outbreak of the First World War. The writer Samuel Lyons, who visited the church in 1815, sketched a rush-bearing garland then

St Michael and All Angels Church, Mottram-in-Longdendale

hanging in the chancel. In 1824 Ebenezer Rhodes visited the church, and noted the annual ritual in which:

> . . . a car or waggon . . . is decorated with a pyramid of rushes, ornamented with wreaths of flowers, and surmounted with a garland, bestrewed with the choicest flowers that the meadows of Glossop Dale can produce . . . Thus prepared, it is drawn through the different parts of the village, preceded by groups of dancers and a band . . . after parading the village the car stops at the church gates; the rushes and flowers are then taken into the church, and strewed amongst the pews and along the floors, and the garlands hung up near the entrance into the chancel in remembrance of the day.

There are many references to rushes and rush-carts in the church wardens' accounts in villages throughout this region; in Peak Forest the ceremony took place on Midsummer eve, whilst at Whitwell, instead of rushes, the hay from a piece of grassland called the Church-close was carted to and spread in the church on the same evening. The origin of these strange ceremonies is undoubtedly older than Christianity, although the Church took over the custom and adapted it for its own use. The last rush-bearing took place in Glossop on the outbreak of the First World War. Today the custom can be seen every August at isolated Macclesfield Forest Chapel, on the western moors, and in Saddleworth and Mossley, in the High Peak region.

The vicarage and churchyard at Old Glossop are said to be haunted by a ghost known as the 'Grey Lady', the wife of a former rector who wears a brown dress and a head-scarf. The present vicarage was built in 1850, away from the site of the previous building, but even so, everyone who has lived in the new building since then, according to local historian Paul Bush, 'has experienced strange happenings from time to time'.

John Knowles, vicar of Glossop between 1865 and 1888, saw a tall slim woman on several occasions during his family's residence in the vicarage, but her face could never be made out clearly. Once Mr Knowles approached the woman, who was standing on the lawn, but as he did so she walked into some shrubs and disappeared. On another occasion the cook awoke one night to find a strange man dressed in a long black robe standing over her. The man was also seen in her kitchen the following Sunday morning. Afterwards, the Knowles were told by Lady Howard that the house was supposed to be haunted by a former vicar, whose wife had murdered him and thrown

114

his body into a well; there is no record of such an event in the church records, and it is thought that Lady Howard may have been having some fun at the expense of the new vicar.

Simmondley Hall, an old manor house south-west of the town, also had a ghost at one time. This restless spirit was of a former occupant of the hall who, it was believed, had hidden a cache of treasure on the premises, the site of which was haunted by a ghostly white horse who would gallop around the hall at night. The elusive treasure, however, was never found. Nearby Coombes House was also haunted, with tales of strange noises and unexplained fires. One writer describes how the building was constructed from stone brought from the remains of the 'Haunted House' which stood at one time on the Monk's Road, an isolated spot where the ghosts of British warriors appear on certain nights of the year.

The name Longdendale, once used to describe a ward of the Royal Forest of the Peak, now refers to the valley of the River Etherow, a tributary of the Mersey. Etherow is a Celtic name, and some authorities believe that the river acted as a boundary between the powerful tribes known as the Cornovii and the Brigantes, before the Romans arrived in Longdendale. The Cornovii inhabited Cheshire, and their name may refer to the horned god of the Celts, Cernunnos; the Brigantes were a strong confederation of warlike tribes who dominated most of what is now the north of England, including the Peak District, where the hill fort on Mam Tor may have been their military strongpoint.

At Gamesley, a western suburb of Glossop, are the remains of the Roman military base of Ardotalia, now known as Melandra Castle. Melandra, deserted by the Roman authorities around AD 155, was one of the small military bases set up by the Roman general Agricola, to garrison the Pennine region, and stands on a ridge of high ground above the River Etherow in the shadow of the native stronghold of Mouselow Hill.

One of the earliest traditions of the neighbourhood tells of a great battle which took place between the advancing Roman armies and the native tribes, which is believed to have been the last great conflict between Britons and Romans in this part of the country. Before the conflict, the Druids are said to have sacrificed the beautiful Nesta, daughter of the British chief, to the gods in the hope of victory. The stone pillars on Ludworth Moor, of medieval date and known as Robin Hood's Picking Rods, were at one time believed to be the remains of the Druid altar where sacrifices were made before the battle. Folklore tells how the Britons then gathered their forces on the rugged gritstone edge known as Coombes Rocks, south-west of Glossop. However, they were drawn to nearby Ludworth Moor by the Romans, where despite great acts of bravery, they were annihilated, deserted by their gods and crushed under the heel of the invader.

The British dead, including Edas, their chief, are said to be buried in the barrows still to be seen on Ludworth Moor, where the Romans erected an altar to victory. In *Legends of Longdendale* Middleton gives the old legend, still told by locals, that:

> . . . it is said that at certain seasons of the year, when the moonlight falls upon the Coombes Rocks, the ghosts of the ancient heroes marshall on the battlefield, waving in phantom hands their phantom axes, as though ready for the coming of the Roman foe. Thus they heap eternal vigil over the wild land they loved of old.

The defeated Britons no doubt retreated to the strongholds of the moors and hills of the High Peak after their defeat by the Romans. One of their fortresses may have been Mouselow or 'Castle Hill', on

Mouselow Hill, Glossop – a sacred place in local legend

116

the north-west outskirts of Glossop, a prominent vantage-point commanding the western approaches to Longdendale Valley. Aerial photography and excavation has produced evidence of an Iron Age fortification on the hill, and a new dig in the 1980s concluded that there were four main phases of occupation, beginning with a Bronze Age burial mound which was superseded by Iron Age earthworks and a Norman castle. The excavators also found water sources on the hill, as well as 'the residue from a small pond or spring', which may have been sacred in pagan times.

In the eighteenth century Bernard Howard, the twelfth Duke of Norfolk, commissioned the building of a small Catholic chapel on the hilltop. This plan was abandoned for unknown reasons, although it is said the workmen broke through into 'something', downed tools and refused to carry on. Rumour has it that a number of mysterious Celtic carvings and stone heads of a cult nature were discovered by the workmen, leading to the building work being abandoned for superstitious reasons, and the hill being planted with trees.

The 'Mouselow Stones' (as they later became known) were removed from the hill in 1840 when land was being cleared for the construction of a Methodist chapel by the vicar of Hadfield, the Revd George Marsden, who built them into the gable end of his house in the village. Later in the nineteenth century, the stones were removed from Hadfield by the Duke of Norfolk, who presented them to the Glossop Antiquarian Society; now they are arranged as part of an archway in Buxton Museum. Antiquarians who examined them at the time pronounced them to be early Anglo-Saxon, with the weird symbols 'representing the river of life, the wind blowing from the four quarters of the earth, Thoth, one of their gods, and other objects which they worshipped'.

The interpretation of the 'Mouselow Stones' has led to much controversy as the stones (originally eight in number, with a further two coming to light in 1986 after local publicity) appear to be of varying ages and style. The carvings include a crude depiction of the Celtic horned god, strange 'shadow figures', phallic symbols and a striking stone head carved in the Celtic tradition. Some of the archaeologists who studied the carvings believe them to be the remains of a Romano-British pagan shrine, and Buxton Museum's display states that they are 'of Celtic Iron Age origin, and may have belonged to larger groups of carvings of cult significance'.

Many similar carved stone heads, some of medieval origin, others dating back to the pagan Celtic era, have been found in the Glossop area. Often the carvings are built into field walls and houses, or have been dug out of topsoil in gardens; but whatever their origin, local folklore invests some of them with magical properties. The excavator of the Mouselow sites, Glynis Reeve, was surprised to discover the existence of strong local feelings about certain stones which were regarded as 'sacred'; and she wrote that 'there has been a stone head cult associated with Glossop for centuries. Whether the Mouselow stones are associated with that cult is uncertain, but they have succeeded in arousing fear and hostility locally'. At the time of the excavation, the team of archaeologists working on Mouselow Hill received harassment from several anxious local people who turned up on site asking who they were, what they were doing and why they were doing it. Weird telephone calls were received in the middle of the night, with anonymous callers giving vague threats abouts the 'Old Ways' and horned figures.

Confirmation of the continuity of belief from the Celtic past is the existence in the High Peak district of a community which still believes in the pagan gods. Dr Anne Ross, an expert in Celtic religion, has written how in 1977 her ethnographic research brought her into contact with a community based in the Longdendale region, who hold beliefs which they describe as 'Celtic', and who closely protect their family-inherited oral traditions and beliefs by means of the 'Guardian of the Old Ways'.

According to Roy Davies, producer of the BBC's *Timewatch* programme, the community is made up of 200 to 500 people 'on scattered farms and small-holdings' in the Longdendale area. In 1977 he described how:

> . . . they believe in the old Celtic gods and goddesses, and their religion is tied to the fertility of the earth. They have fertility rites in the sense that they practised in the past, rites which ensure the fertility of their crops. There is no question today of rituals with sexual overtones, which may have been included in the past. I could not get as close to them as I would have wanted, as there was very much a clamp-down on questions about their leaders, on where they met and what they actually did when they met.

Anne Ross was told by the spokesman for the group how 'stone heads are buried in the valley, wells garlanded with simple bunches of flowers at Beltain [the first day of May], the threefold mother goddess is known and acknowledged, and the Beltain bonfires lit on every farm'. In a documentary, screened by the BBC in 1986, the

'Guardian of the Old Ways' described how it is believed locally that 'the head is the most important part of the body', and was used as an old form of protection against witchcraft. These beliefs had been transmitted from generation to generation, and are similar to traditions surviving elsewhere in the Yorkshire Pennines, where carved heads placed in house gables were said to act as talismans, protecting the house from evil influence.

The Mouselow saga demonstrates how Longdendale, despite the encroachment of the twentieth century, remains a brooding, introverted valley where old traditions die hard. Rumours about strange happenings on the moors, including stories of the meetings of withcraft covens, have been common over the years, and despite exaggerated newspaper reports, it is known that covens both black and white still operate in the area. The fourteenth-century Woodhead Chapel, incongruously sited on a bank between the Woodhead road and the high moorland above, was desecrated by self-styled Satanists in the late 1970s; this act of vandalism has added to the reputation of the area, although as Rex Bellamy notes in *The Peak District Companion*: 'Any woman cavorting about Longdendale naked would swiftly find herself in an intensive care unit'!

Near Woodhead is the site of Crowden Hall, dismantled by Manchester Corporation in 1937, but still the haunt, in local folklore, of a headless horseman. The hall was built in the seventeenth century by the Hatfield family, one of whom was the criminal and vagabond Thomas Hatfield, executed at Carlisle in 1803. His death, so it is said, was prophesied in his youth by a local astrologer, an old man who predicted the future by consulting the stars and a skull. He had told Hatfield that he would meet his end in Cumberland, and was in the end proved correct.

Longdendale Valley was once forested, and old traditions tell of a 'mighty forest, whose trees were so thick that the squirrels could leap from branch to branch from Mottram to Woodhead'; later a string of hamlets grew up in the valley, including the thriving communities of Crowden and Woodhead. Despite the changes which accompanied the building of the reservoirs in the 1930s, the eastern section between Tintwistle and Woodhead has always been dominated by the dark moorland heights of Black Hill and Bleaklow. The valley today is notable as the route of the trans-Pennine traffic on the A628 Woodhead road, which is accompanied by a string of five reservoirs, a railway line, and long stretches of high-tension electricity pylons.

Ghostly happenings have been reported for centuries in the valley

– phantom Roman soldiers, strange lights on the moors, and witchcraft. As well as the witches, 'Owd Nick' himself is said to have made his appearance, thwarted as ever by the ingenuity of his human adversaries.

Thomas Middleton, writing in 1906, described how Longdendale 'has always been noted for the number of its inhabitants devoted to the study of magic arts'. Mossey Lea, near Glossop, was 'notable as having been the home of a great magician who dwelt there in the olden time, who was renowned far and wide – he was, perhaps, the most powerful and learned of all magicians since the time of Merlin'. One version of this story tells how one day the great magician – whose reputation grew so much that he was called Dr Faust, after the famous German wizard – was visited by the Devil himself. Confident of his powers, the doctor challenged his adversary to a race over the Roman road on the moors. Inevitably, the Devil was able to outrun the clever magician, but putting his horse to the gallop the doctor remembered that he had to cross a stream of clear running water, and upon doing so the Devil lost all claims to the doctor's soul, as it is well known that evil spirits cannot abide or cross running water. The name of a section of the Roman road linking Brough, near Castleton, with Melandra at Glossop, is to this day known as Doctor's Gate, after the legend. Devil's Dyke, north of the Snake road, is said to be where the Devil scratched a huge gash across the moorland to rent his anger.

The Devil is also credited with the naming of a hairpin bend on the minor road which connects Glossop with Woodhead, where it crosses Ogden Clough. The 'Devil's Elbow', as this dangerous bend is known, took its name from a story of two lovers who were fleeing from the Devil, with whom they had broken a pact. His Satanic Majesty, however, gained on them rapidly, and just as it appeared certain that he would catch them: '. . . he put out his hand to touch the maid, a strange light appeared in the sky and a voice called out the one word "Hold". The devil staggered as if he had been shot, and when he recovered the light had vanished, and with it the maiden and her lover . . .'

The story told by Middleton in 1906 adds that the lovers:

. . . were never seen again, but the legends say they were made perfectly happy by the fairies, and that they still haunt the banks of the Etherow at certain seasons of the year in the forms of two white swans . . . As for the devil he received a shock. At the moment the light appeared, his right arm had been bent at the elbow for the purpose of seizing hold of his prey, but lo! when his victims had disappeared, he found that the powers that had delivered them from him had turned his right arm into stone. Not a muscle of it could he move, it would not bend, it was worse than useless . . . he tore the arm out by the roots and left it there – the elbow showing prominently over Longdendale. And that is how the great rock known as the Devil's Elbow came to be perched high up above the Etherow Valley.

The Devil's Elbow, Longdendale

The Devil's Elbow has retained its eerie reputation in modern times. John Davies, an old railwayman who lives in one of the few remaining cottages in this part of the valley, has described how:

. . . the only encounter I've had happened one bright moonlit night as I was on my motorbike on a section of the road known as the Devil's Elbow. The moon lit everything up as bright as day and as I rounded the corner, level with the farm, something sort of told me to stop. I stopped and saw something coming across the road, really peculiar, like a whale. It came slowly across in front of me, and it

121

had a head just like a whale and a white eye, with a black pupil going round and round. I couldn't see through it and had to stop right in front of it. It didn't frighten me but I had a queer sensation. It was like a massive black slug sliding across t'road and up to t'moor. It disappeared and I got off and had a look. But there was nothing there. I've been over there thousands of times and never seen anything like that before.

Mr Davies has described to the writer how another man had a strange experience at the same spot when returning home from Manchester late one night. He had the sensation that something huge was following behind him, dragging itself along the bank up to the moor. Mr Davies adds that 'I'd believe anything about this area, it's a weird place at night. There have always been rumours about ghosts and I've heard the stories about the ghosts of Roman soldiers.'

Another ghostly black shape appeared at one time in the western stretch of Longdendale Valley, the scene of a haunting by a 'phantom lorry'. This up-to-date apparition was said to frequent a stretch of the A57 Manchester to Sheffield road between the towns of Hyde and Mottram-in-Longdendale. During the years 1929–1930 over sixteen major accidents occurred there, including three deaths and twenty-five serious injuries. The local coroner became so concerned about the strange series of unsolved accidents that he took his jury to the spot at midnight to look for clues! The phantom lorry was the focus of much newspaper speculation at the time, and many residents came forward with strange tales of phantom footsteps being heard around houses just before accidents took place, but the mystery remains unsolved to this day.

Legend says that the ghosts of Roman soldiers appear on Bleaklow at the first full moon of spring, and there have been a string of these reports from walkers on the Pennine way. The stretch of path linking the Roman forts of Anavio (Brough) and Melandra Castle at Glossop is the focus of a persistent legend which tells of the spirits of marching Roman legions. David Frith, of Glossop Mountain Rescue Team, told the *Manchester Evening News* in March 1979 how, the previous summer, wardens working for the National Park had spoken to walkers who had seen two or three ghostly Roman soldiers on Bleaklow.

In *High Peak* Eric Byne and Geoffrey Sutton tell how one blustery night in 1932 four climbers arrived in a breathless condition at Crookstone Barn, near Jaggers Clough on Kinder Scout, and told how:

> . . . they had lain on the heather near the thirteenth-century Hope
> Cross, and watched as a Roman legion marched past on the lane.
> They later described the distinctive long curved shields of the
> legionnaires and their curious helmets to perfection.

The prevalence of Roman ghost stories in this part of Longdendale
has led to speculation about the possible existence of a Roman road
linking the Snake Pass with Longdendale, one theory being that part
of it went over the top of Shining Clough near Torside Castle.

The Longdendale Lights

The greatest ghost story of recent years is without a doubt the
mystery of 'Longdendale Lights', which are said to appear from time
to time on the remote western face of Bleaklow. Walkers and
residents have reported seeing a powerful beam of light – rather like
a searchlight – in the area of Bramah Edge and Clough Edge, beyond
the Torside Reservoir. Other reports described a string of moving,
elusive and eventually fading lights that appear on the remote,
craggy gritstone heights of Bleaklow beyond Shining Clough, in the
area of a curious natural hillock known as Torside Castle.

Rescue teams have been called out on many occasions, because
ramblers on these desolate moors are always advised to carry torches
for emergency use. But no one, nor any clue of any kind, has ever been
found which might explain the source of these lights. Philip Shaw, the
Accident Record Officer of the Peak District Mountain Rescue
Organisation, has said that between them, the seven Peak District
rescue teams are called out at least once a year by people who see
inexplicable lights on the hills and assume that walkers are in
distress. This has been going on for at least twenty years, but no
explanation has ever been found: 'during the 1960s the National Park
Warden . . . who lived at Crowden in Longdendale quite often saw
lights – not flares – in the vicinity of Clough Edge above Torside
Reservoir. On occasions these were investigated, but nothing was
found.'

In the summer of 1970, Mrs Barbara Drabble, a trainee teacher,
experienced the mystery lights of Longdendale first-hand whilst
returning home to Crowden on the Woodhead Pass. In the *Peak Park
News,* Spring 1972 issue, she describes her sighting in graphic terms:

Torside Reservoir, Longdendale Valley

The stark north side of Bleaklow – home of the 'Longdendale Lights'

If you know the Woodhead road you will know that from Tintwistle to Woodhead on the left-hand side of the road is bleak moorland and on the right the reservoirs, a railway line and then the stark forbidding north side of Bleaklow. This is indeed a very impressive sight very late at night with the moon shining and the cold black outline of the mountain towering over the reservoir. Especially when it is common knowledge that a legion of Roman soldiers tramp over the moor regularly on such nights.

It was on one such night one year ago last July that I was driving alone along this road, stone-cold sober I might add. It was past midnight but still quite warm and I was driving along admiring the view, thinking this must be the most beautiful place in the world to live, when suddenly from somewhere on Bleaklow there shone the most brilliant blue light. It lit up all the bottom half of Bleaklow, all the railway, the reservoirs and about a two-mile stretch of the road. As I drove into it the car went icy cold and I quickly put the window up. The air appeared to vibrate. The light had the same piercing brightness as lightning but this light lasted some three or four minutes. It then disappeared as suddenly as it had come. I was terrified. I asked around the neighbourhood but no one admitted seeing it and appeared reluctant even to discuss the matter.

Then, last July, one warm summer night, everyone in Crowden Hostel was amazed to see the whole hostel lit up by a strange bluish light emanating from somewhere on Bleaklow. It lasted three minutes, twenty five seconds and lit up half Bleaklow, all the railway, the reservoir and about a two-mile stretch of the road. This time rescue teams went out to search. This time locals reluctantly admitted to seeing it and to having seen it on previous occasions. The large search lamp used by rescuers looked like a small torch on Bleaklow when viewed from the hostel. It is therefore impossible to credit a light of the magnitude of the one seen. The search parties found nothing and saw nobody. All was quiet and warm with only a faint mist.

Since the early 1970s, there have been several further sightings of the Longdendale Lights; in October 1978, local climber David Frith, a member of the Glossop Mountain Rescue Team, described to a *Manchester Evening News* reporter how he first heard of the lights in 1972, and since then:

. . . there have been frequent calls about them to the rescue team. The last sighting I heard of was in October last year, when they

125

looked like a string of walkers carrying torches. They drifted about and then faded away. Other times it's been like a searchlight coming out of the hillside.'

One of the most recent reports was in February 1982, when the Glossop team were called out at 7.15 pm after a sighting of a 'green flare' rising over the moors west of Torside Clough. Subsequently, twenty-five rescue team members, together with three National Park rangers spent three hours searching the desolate peat groughs between Torside Clough, Bramah Edge and Mossylee. The search went on until around midnight, but no explanation for the light could be found. A spokesman said afterwards that 'over the years many stories have been told about mysterious lights on the south side of Longdendale and ghostly Roman legions in the vicinity of Torside Castle'. He added that:

... if it had happened once the sightings would have been put down to the work of a prankster, but when it happened with gaps of four or five years between sightings this explanation became unlikely. We are all completely in the dark – I don't believe in ghosts, but there's something up there. It happens too often to be just chance.

Strange ghostly lights have also been spotted by motorists on the A635 'Isle of Skye' road between Holmfirth and Greenfield, which crosses one of the most remote landscapes in the Pennines, reaching almost 1,500 feet above sea level at its highest point. The road is surrounded with desolate peat bogs, with Wessenden Moor to the north, and Black Hill to the south, stretching as far as the eye can see into Derbyshire. The region is the scene, at Saddleworth Moor to the west, of the infamous Moors Murders case, and it is little wonder that given its reputation, the moorlands are said to be haunted. Just to the north of A635, just before the road begins to descend into Saddleworth, are a group of rocks known as the 'Boggart Stones'. 'Boggart' is the local name for a ghost or apparition, and the name may refer to a spot haunted in the past. To the north, Running Hill Head Farm on the edge of the moors is haunted by a number of ghosts, including 'curious lights' which have 'no specific form, they were never very bright and they moved about the bedroom like wisps of phosphorescent smoke.'

One misty night in August 1975, a motorist from Manchester was confronted by a 'huge glowing egg-shaped object as big as a double-decker bus' at Wessenden Head, the highest point on the moorland road. The man said later that 'it tapered towards the back like a pear or an egg, and looked fluorescent or transparent with a very bright light inside . . . it took a minute to cross the road, and I watched it altogether for about four minutes at close range'.

Many others have reported similar lights and ghostly shapes in the area; a policeman who used to patrol the lonely road has described seeing 'a bright light which zipped sideways over the bog for 300 yards; and circular light like a saucer-shaped spotlight which rose noiselessly into the sky'. Mountain Rescue Teams twice turned out from Crowden in the autumn of 1975 to investigate 'flare-type' lights on the moors at Wessenden. They found nothing.

Typical of the experiences reported from these lonely moors is the following, reported by Philip O'Brien, who was crossing the moors with two friends one dark night in November 1980:

We had just left the lights of Saddleworth behind and had just turned the sharp corner at the top of the climb – almost parallel to where the Moors Murders took place. Suddenly, to the left of us a mysterious light appeared, travelling across the moor. It was almost three foot off the ground and travelled at a constant speed from left to right. It never changed its speed or direction, and the contours of the land (formed by peat groughs) made no difference to it. It passed 100 yards in front of the car and disappeared over the moor in the direction of Cloudberry Knoll; of its size I would say it looked like a dipped car headlight – it was silent and at the time there were no other cars in sight.

Bibliography

Addy, S. O.	*Folk-tales and Superstitions* (EP Publishing, 1973; originally published 1895)
Andrews, Dr Mary	*Long Ago in Peakland* (Loughborough, 1948)
Barnatt, John	*Stone Circles of the Peak* (Turnstone Books, 1978)
Bellamy, Rex	*The Peak District Companion* (David and Charles, 1981)
Cameron, Kenneth	*The Place-Names of Derbyshire* (Cambridge University Press, 1959)
Clarke, D. and Wilson, R.	*Strange Sheffield: Legends, Folklore and Mysteries of Hallamshire* (Sheffield, 1987)
Daniel, Clarence	*Ghosts of Derbyshire* (Dalesman, 1973) *Haunted Derbyshire* (Dalesman, 1975) *Derbyshire Traditions* (Dalesman, 1975) *Derbyshire Customs* (Dalesman, 1976)
Jewitt, Llewellyn	*Derbyshire Ballads* (London, 1867)
McGregor, A. A.	*The Ghost Book* (Robert Hale, 1955)
Merrill, John	*Derbyshire Folklore* (JNM, 1988)
Naylor, Peter J.	*Celtic Derbyshire* (Derby, 1983)
Porteous, Crichton	*The Ancient Customs of Derbyshire* (Derbyshire Countryside, 1976)
Rhodes, Ebenezer	*Peak Scenery* (1824)
Rickman, R. and Nown, G.	*Mysterious Derbyshire* (Dalesman, 1977)
Rodgers, Frank	*Curiosities of the Peak District* (Moorland, 1979)
Smith, Roland	*First and Last* (Peak Park, 1978)
Turner, W. M.	*Romances of the Peak* (London, 1901)
Warrender, Keith	*High Peak Faces and Places* (Oldham, 1978)
Whitaker, P. D.	*Early settlement in Derbyshire* (Dalesman, 1974)
Wood, William	*Tales and Traditions of the High Peak* (Richard Keen, 1952)